P9-BYT-073

THE OFFICIAL
POLITICALLY
CORRECT
DICTIONARY
AND HANDBOOK

UPDATED! NEW ENTRIES!

THE OFFICIAL
POLITICALLY
CORRECT
DICTIONARY
AND HANDBOOK

HENRY BEARD AND CHRISTOPHER CERF

Produced in Conjunction with The American Hyphen Society

Designed by ROBERT BULL DESIGN

Contributing Illustrators:
LAUREN ATTINELLO AND TOM BRANNON

VILLARD BOOKS | NEW YORK
1994

Copyright ©1992 by Henry Beard and Christopher Cerf
All rights reserved under International and Pan-American Copyright
Conventions. Published in the United States by Villard Books, a division
of Random House, Inc., New York and simultaneously in Canada by
Random House of Canada Limited, Toronto.
Villard Books is a registered trademark of Random House, Inc.

All text and illustration permissions and acknowledgments can be found
on pages 191–92.

Library of Congress Cataloging-in-Publication Data

Beard, Henry.
    The official politically correct dictionary and handbook / Henry
    Beard and Christopher Cerf; designed by Robert Bull Design; con-
    tributing illustrators, Lauren Attinello and Tom Brannon.—New
    updated ed.
            p.   cm.
    "Produced in conjunction with the American Hyphen Society"—
    CIP t.p.
    ISBN 0-679-74944-6
            1. American wit and humor. 2. Euphemism—Humor. 3. Lan-
guage and culture—Humor. 4. Political correctness—Humor I. Cerf,
Christopher. II. Title.
PN6162.B372 1994
818'.5402—dc20   93-29964

The text of this book is set in Stempel Garamond.
Manufactured in the United States of America on acid-free paper
9876

Updated Edition

For the former Donna Ellen Cooperman,
who, after a courageous yearlong battle
through the New York State court system,
won the right to be known as
Donna Ellen Cooperperson

"It was intended that when Newspeak had been adopted once and for all and Oldspeak forgotten, a heretical thought...should be literally unthinkable, at least so far as thought is dependent on words."
—George Orwell, *1984*

WATCH WHAT YOU SAY!
(A BRIEF GUIDE TO USING THIS BOOK)

Professor Roderick Nash of the University of California at Santa Barbara thought he was up on the new appropriateness. He had heard all about how it was disrespectful to household nonhuman animals to call them "pets," and knew that a more correct term was "animal companions." So one day, he decided to tell his environmental ethics class what he thought was a harmless little joke. "I wonder if the women who pose for *Penthouse* magazine want to be called '*Penthouse* animal companions,'" he mused.

Well, you've probably already figured out what happened next. Several alert members of Professor Nash's class filed a formal sexual-harassment charge against him. "Maybe this will make more people aware and other faculty watch what they say," explained Susan Rode, one of the students who signed the complaint.

Now, we don't want to appear immodest, but frankly, if Professor Nash had owned a copy of *The Official Politically Correct Dictionary and Handbook*, he would never have uttered such a disastrously inappropriate remark. And don't think for a minute something similar couldn't happen to you. Indeed, whether you're an oppressor or victim (or aren't even sure which), you, too, desperately need this book to survive in the be-sensitive-or-else nineties.

The Official Politically Correct Dictionary and Handbook is divided into handy sections that will tell you what's OK to say to whom, what isn't, and why. There's even a section that tells you what opinions and concepts are acceptable, and which ones you're just going to have to discard. Here are the exciting details:

PART I: A Dictionary of Politically Correct (PC) Terms and Phrases, From ableism to Zeus-as-rapist presents the basics. Use it to look up unfamiliar concepts such as "phallocentrism," "handi-capable," and "melanin impoverished" and see what they mean. Part I is also particularly helpful when you want to find out what oppressions you've been subjected to, and what to call the perpetrators.

PART II: A Politically Incorrect/Politically Correct Dictionary is a thesaurus and bilingual dictionary combined. You'll find it invaluable when you want to look up the outmoded, offensive terms you've *been* using, like "black," "prisoner," "fat," and "old"—and replace them with up-to-date, unexceptionable equivalents, such as "African-American," "client of the correctional system," "possessing an alternative body image," and "chronologically gifted." Once you've mastered Part II, we guarantee you won't offend anyone—except those who *deserve* to be offended!

PART III: Other Suspect Words, Concepts, and "Heroes" to Be Avoided and/or Discarded takes you beyond "incorrect" speech and language to an exploration of the core thoughts, customs, and beliefs—e.g., individual liberties, freedom of speech, dating, the domestication of animals—that corrupted our culture in the first place. Eliminate these items from your belief system—indeed, "belief systems" themselves are included in our catalog of suspect concepts to be avoided and/or discarded—and you'll be well on your way to mastering the rules of the new sensitivity.

PART IV: Know Your Oppressor: A Bilingual Glossary of Bureaucratically Suitable (BS) Language is an indispensable guide to the unique brand of correct-speak used by our corporate, political, and military leaders. You'll learn here, for example, that it's not acid rain, it's "poorly buffered precipitation"; that one never lies, one just "strategically misrepresents"; that "saturation bombing" is merely "terrain alteration"; that the *Challenger* incident was not an accident but an "anomaly"; and that there are literally dozens of handy ways of saying "You're fired" without ever having to use those words.

Well, there you have it. In a moment you'll be turning this page and beginning your reeducation. The importance of your learning—and conforming to—the rules spelled out, entry by entry, in *The Official Politically Correct Dictionary and Handbook* cannot be overemphasized. For, as linguists Edward Sapir and Benjamin Lee Whorf suspected as early as the 1940s—and postmodernist theory has confirmed—language is not merely the mirror of our society; it is *the* major force in "constructing" what we perceive as "reality." With this in mind, it's easy to see why so many reformers have forsworn a unified assault on such distracting side issues as guaranteeing equal pay for equal work; eliminating unemployment, poverty, and homelessness; counteracting the inordinate influence of moneyed interests on the electoral system; and improving the dismal state of American education, all in order to devote their energies to correcting the fundamental linguistic inequities described in these pages.

Sure, helping you—and each and every one of our readers—was an important reason why we joined forces with the American Hyphen Society to create *The Official Politically Correct Dictionary and Handbook.* But frankly, we also had a bigger goal in mind—a goal perhaps best expressed by Betsy Warland in her poem "the breasts refuse." "[I]f we change language," Warland wrote, "we change everything." We invite all America—and (to quote the New York State Social Studies Review and Development Committee) "the peoples who person it"—to join us in our struggle.

—HENRY BEARD and CHRISTOPHER CERF

A NOTE ABOUT THE EXPANDED, UPDATED EDITION

When *The Official Politically Correct Dictionary and Handbook* was first published, it never occurred to us that, scarcely a year later, we would find it necessary to rush into print an updated, expanded edition. But, accelerated by the relentless press of events, language reform has proceeded at a pace that we at The American Hyphen Society find not only gratifying, but truly amazing. For example:

- The display of widespread community dissatisfaction that swept Los Angeles following the Rodney King verdict has given us a long-over-due new phrase, "nontraditional shoppers," to replace the pathetically insensitive term "looters."

- The New York Zoological Society has finally come to its senses and removed the word "zoo"—sullied by its inclusion in such phrases as "This place is a total zoo!"—from the names of its facilities in the Bronx, Manhattan, Brooklyn, and Queens. Henceforth, these attractions will be known as "wildlife preservation centers." (The society has also changed its *own* name: to the far more appropriate—and snappy—"NYZS/The Wildlife Preservation Society.")

- And, in mounting its historic 1993 Biennial Exhibition, the Whitney Museum of American Art has made "pathetic aesthetic" a household word, and would also have established ineptitude and lack of originality as the new standards by which all art should henceforth be judged, had not "standards" and "judgment" themselves become obsolete and unacceptable concepts.

Developments like these, and the emergence of such significant coinages as *cultural tourism, custody suite, feelism, femmchismo, ferms, herms, merms, msterbation, pedal sizism,* and *phallogocentrism,* have made your purchase and dedicated use of this revised volume (even if you already own a copy of the original edition) nothing short of essential. You'll thank us, and you're welcome!

—HENRY BEARD and CHRISTOPHER CERF

A DICTIONARY OF POLITICALLY CORRECT (PC) TERMS AND PHRASES

From **ableism** to **Zeus-as-rapist**

Ableism. The Smith College Office of Student Affairs defines this as "oppression of the differently abled, by the temporarily able."[1] See also: **differently abled; temporarily able.**

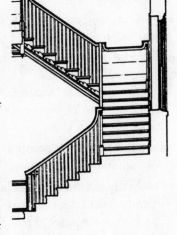

Stairs, an example of **ableist** *architecture.*

ableist language. Language offensive, or insensitive, to the differently abled.[2] Kirsten Hearn, in a letter to the feminist journal *Spare Rib,* offered as examples of ableist language the use of statements such as "I see what you mean" and "What is your view on this point?" instead of "I understand what you mean" and "What is your opinion?"

acceptional child. A child with a learning disability. "Acceptional" is an alternate spelling for "exceptional," coined to emphasize the "special" child's need for acceptance.[3] See also: **differently abled; exceptional; handi-capable; special.**

accommodationism. The belief that showing respect for, or compromising with, one's oppressors may, at least on occasion, be productive.[4] Example: *It was* **accommodationist** *of Barbara Smith to write, in "Notes for Yet Another Paper on Black Feminism," that "it is safe to assume that 99.44 percent of all white men are racists and sexists," thereby admitting that 0.56 percent of them may not be.*[5]

acquaintance rape. A term defined by a Swarthmore College training manual as spanning "a spectrum of incidents and behaviors ranging from crimes legally defined as rape to verbal harassment and inappropriate innuendo."[6] Example: *Who was that lady*

I saw you with last night? That was no lady, that was an **acquaintance rape** *survivor!*

actron. A non-gender-specific substitute for the words "actor" and "actress," modeled after the trendsetting term **waitron**.[7]

additional preparation. A nonjudgmental educational term for "remedial instruction." The word "remedial" is unacceptable because it "blames" students by implying they have a deficiency which needs to be corrected.[8] See also: **advanced readiness seminars**.

advanced readiness seminars. Special classes for students who need **additional preparation**.[9]

adverbially premodified adjectival lexical unit. The most frequently used linguistic form in the construction of culturally appropriate language. "Physically inconvenienced," "involuntarily leisured," "ethically disoriented," and, of course, "politically correct" are all examples of adverbially premodified adjectival lexical units.[10]

African-American. The Smith College Office of Student Affairs defines "African-American" as "one of several concepts that refer to those citizens of the United States who are of African descent."[11] It is generally considered more appropriate than "black" because it implies a connection with the home continent and because, as linguistics expert Robert B. Moore puts it, "the symbolism of white as positive and black as negative [is] pervasive in our culture."[12] Nonetheless, the term "African-American" should be used with caution, warn the Fellows [sic] of the University of Missouri Journalism School's Multicultural Management Program, since "it may be objectionable to those persons preferring black."[13]

African-American worldview. Florida A&M professors Yvonne R. Bell, Cathy L. Bouie, and Joseph A. Baldwin report that, contrary to assimilationist assumptions embodied in what they call "the Eurocentric/cultural deprivation framework," African-Americans have their own distinct cultural orientation, or "worldview," defined by two guiding principals: "oneness with nature" and "survival of the group." Among the cultural values they cite as "consistent with the basic principles of the African-American worldview" are interdependence, cooperation, unity, mutual responsibility, and reconciliation.[14] For Ms. Bell, Ms. Bouie, and Mr. Baldwin's definition of the *Euro*-American worldview, see **Euro-American worldview**.

Afrocentrism. A multifaceted movement whose aim is to research, analyze, interpret, and teach history from an African point of view and to dislodge "Western" civilization from its self-appointed position, in the words of Temple University professor Bayo Oyebade, as "the yardstick by which every other culture is defined." The activities that constitute Afrocentrism cover a remarkably diverse intellectual and political spectrum, ranging from scholarly research on early African cultures, through attempts to modify or supplant current school curricula, to Dr. Leonard Jeffries's startlingly innovative theory of "sun people" and "ice people." Afrocentrism's aim, Oyebade writes passionately (but not gender-inclusively), is nothing less than "the humanization of the universe by the Black man."[15] See also: **ice people; sun people**.

ageism. "Oppression of the young and the old, by young adults and the middle-aged, in the belief that others are 'incapable' or unable to take care of themselves" (as defined by the Smith College Office of Student Affairs).[16] Example: *The Non-**Ageist** Press's fall book list included such titles as* The Senior Citizen and the Sea, Longer-Living Yeller, *and* The Rime of the Chronologically Gifted Mariner.

Alaskan native. See: **Native Alaskan**.

Aleut. See: **Native Alaskan**.

alphabetism. The widespread and arbitrary privileging of persons, institutions, and nations whose names begin with letters that come early in the alphabet, and the oppression of those whose names do not.[17]

alternative body image, person with an.   An obese person; a person of size; a person of substance.[18] See also: **larger-than-average citizen.**

alternative dentation.   False teeth.[19]

alternatively concise.   Verbose, long-winded.[20] Example: *Bill Clinton has a well-deserved reputation for delivering* **alternatively concise** *speeches.*

alternatively schooled.   Uneducated; illiterate.[21]

ambigenic.   Applying fairly and equally to both females and males. A positive, upbeat substitute for the term "nonsexist," which is deemed "negative" by a growing number of critics because it talks about what it isn't, rather than what it is.[22] See also: **epicene.**

animal companion.   Pet.[23] Ingrid Newkirk, national director of People for the Ethical Treatment of Animals, prefers "companion animal."[24] According to *U.S. News & World Report,* both these terms are coming into disrepute because they are **anthropocentric;** i.e., they imply that the human role in the relationship is somehow superior. Proponents of this point of view suggest such alternatives as "friend" or **protec-**

A prewoman and her **animal companion.**

tor. The word **companion,** standing alone, is also recommended in some circles, but, since the term may also be used as a nonheterosexist, gender-free substitute for "lover," caution is advised.

animality.   Professor Vincent Scully of Yale University suggests this as an improvement upon the word "humanity," which he finds exceptionable because it arbitrarily excludes other species.[25] See: **speciesism**.

animal lookism. The tendency of less-than-fully-committed animal rights advocates to protect "adorable" species, such as bunnies and puppies, while ignoring the equally valid claims of less "attractive" creatures such as rats and reptiles. According to the Animal Liberation Front, "Cuteness should not be a factor."[26]

The rat, a voiceless victim of **animal lookism.**

anthropocentrism. The belief that human animals are superior to nonhuman animals and therefore have the right to enslave, experiment upon, and eat them.[27] Example: *It was grossly* **anthropocentric** *of Doctor Louis Pasteur to experiment with cattle and sheep, even if his vaccinations did happen to save hundreds of millions of human animal lives.*

anti-ismizationism. A doctrine inspired by the writings of self-appointed linguistic purists Alan and Theresa von Altendorf, who insist that such concepts as "ableism," "ageism," "fatism," and "heightism" serve no purpose beyond proving that one can "give credibility to any trendy thought just by adding 'ism' to the end of a word." "We are alarmed by the growing 'ismization' of the language," the von Altendorfs announce in the introduction to their book, *Isms.* "We are also alarmed by the growing 'ization' of the language," they add, "but that's another book."[28] See also: **linguistic purism**.

aroma police. See: **scentism**.

Asian-American. The Smith College Office of Student Affairs defines this as "a self-definition reflecting the common identity, similar treatment, and shared goals of those U.S. citizens of Asian descent." The word "Oriental" is not acceptable, the Smith Office continues, because it was bestowed "by other people"—in this case, by Europeans. "Naming someone is a symbol of the power one has over them to define who they are," the Smith office concludes. "Naming oneself reclaims that power."[29]

assimilationism. The conviction that members of nonempowered groups should forswear the celebration of their Otherness and adopt, or attempt to imitate, the mores and customs of the dominant culture.[30]

A flagrantly **assimilationist** *emblem.*

attention deficit disordered child. A pupil who disrupts a classroom.[31]

aurally inconvenienced. Hard-of-hearing; deaf.[32] Also: **aurally challenged.**

autoeuthanasia. A more sensitive term for "suicide."[33] See also: **spiritually dysfunctional; voluntary death.**

Batchild and **ballchild.** Proposed nonsexist alternatives for "batboy" and "ballboy" cited by University of Illinois linguistics professor Dennis Baron.[34] Example: *"That's not an error—that's a differently fielded grounder!"* exclaimed the batchild *to the* ballchild *as the shortstop bobbled the ball.*

biocentrism. The doctrine that every species has equal intrinsic value and that the planet earth cannot be viewed solely as a resource for human beings.[35] Biocentrism is the central tenet of the so-called **deep ecology** movement, and is typified by the view of John Davis, editor of *Earth First! Journal,* that "eradicating smallpox was wrong. It played an important part in balancing ecosystems."

bioregionalism. The growing movement to replace nation-states with "bioregions"—areas defined by the fact that they share a common ecosystem rather than by artificial (and inherently meaningless) political boundaries. Humans, bioregionalists say, must become part of the natural food chain and water cycle of their bioregion, instead of arrogantly trying to impose their own technological order over nonhuman species.[36] Example: "*My bioregion right or wrong!*" read the ecofascist bumper sticker.

birthmother; birthfather; birthparent. The correct terms for the biological parents of children who have been adopted. Terms such as "real father" and "natural mother," which imply that it is somehow "unreal" or "unnatural" to take another's biological child into one's family, are highly offensive to adoptive parents.[38]

birth name. A less demeaning term for "maiden name," recommended by Val Dumond, author of *The Elements of Nonsexist Usage.*[37]

blacks of the African Diaspora. African-Americans or Caribbean-Americans, for example.[39] Also: **members of the African Diaspora**. See also: **communities of the African Diaspora.**

body decolonization. Becoming a lesbian.[40] See: **decolonization.**

borealocentrism. The implicit belief that the peoples and cultures of the Northern Hemisphere are superior to those of the Southern Hemisphere, characterized by the arbitrary placement of the North Pole at the "top" of the globe.[41]

*A non**borealocentric** globe.*

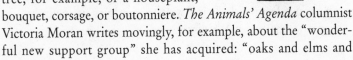

botanical companion. A favorite tree, for example, or a houseplant, bouquet, corsage, or boutonniere. *The Animals' Agenda* columnist Victoria Moran writes movingly, for example, about the "wonderful new support group" she has acquired: "oaks and elms and evergreens, tulips and irises and begonias. These companions are quiet—but not so quiet that listening carefully doesn't let me hear what they have to say."[42] Also: **floral companion.**

A woman and her **botanical companion.**

C **canine-American.** A dog who resides in the United States.[43]

canon, the. The body of Western literary, historical, and political works—written almost exclusively by dead, white, heterosexual, English-speaking, Eurocentric males— that academic traditionalists (also predominantly white and male) still insist on defining as "great." Postmodern critical theory has revealed what many feel should have been obvious all along: that such qualitative judgments are always politically motivated. "There is no such thing as intrinsic merit," Stanley Fish, the head of the English department at Duke University, explains. [44] See also: **noncanonical texts.**

capitalistic patriarchal hegemonic discourse. The means by which the dominant culture and its institutions oppress the marginalized and dispossessed masses. In informal speech, the phrase is often run together as if it were a single word and, according to American Hyphen Society linguist Maryam Mohit, it is more and more frequently being written that way as well: "capitalisticpatriarchalhegemonicdiscourse."[45]

carbocentrism. The belief by carbon-based life-forms that theirs is the best or the only possible basis for the development of intelligent, sentient beings. Carbocentric attitudes and remarks are offensive to silicon-based life forms, even if they live on worlds so remote that any such remarks that happen to be broadcast from Earth at the speed of light will not reach them for millions of years nor be intelligible to them when they do arrive.[46]

centrocentrism. The assumption that positions and opinions echoing the moderate, "middle-of-the-road" viewpoint held by a statistical plurality of any population are somehow superior to those espoused by minority factions; and the accompanying tendency of the dominant culture media to marginalize such factions by characterizing their ideas as "far out," "radical," or "extreme."[47]

cerebrally challenged. Stupid.[48] Example: *"Move it,* **cerebrally challenged***!" shouted the cab driver* .

cerebro-atmospheric individual. The American Hyphen Society's proposed substitute for "airhead," which is characterized by the Multicultural Management Fellows [sic] of the University of Missouri Journalism School (who are dedicated, they inform us, to "turning today's journalists into tomorrow's multicultural newsroom managers") as "an objectionable description, generally aimed at women."[49]

chair. Increasingly the preferred gender-inclusive substitute for "chairman" or "chairwoman," according to usage experts Casey Miller and Kate Swift.[50] Example: *Charlene asked the* **chair** *to table the motion.*

charm-free. Boring.[51] Also: **differently interesting.**

chemically inconvenienced. Under the influence of alcohol or drugs.[52] See also: **sobriety-deprived.**

Chicana/Chicano. The preferred term for women and men, respectively, of Mexican-American descent, created, according to the Smith College Office of Student Affairs, "to reflect their concern about preserving their culture and heritage as opposed to assimilating into the dominant Eurocentric culture of the U.S.A."[53]

chronologically gifted. Old.[54] See also: **experientially enhanced; longer-living; mature; senior; seasoned.**

classism. "The oppression of the working-class and nonpropertied, by the upper and middle class" (as defined by the Smith College Office of Student Affairs).[55]

client of the correctional system. A prisoner.[56] See also: **guest.**

co. See: coself.

collective defamation. *The New York Times* defines this as "the idea that both pornography and hate speech inflict harm not only on the individual taunted by the words or participating in the photo shoot but on all minorities and women." The concept of collective defamation is the basis of new legislation, proposed by a coalition of anti-pornography feminists and anti-defamation scholars, which would permit any individual who feels victimized by speech or images she or he deems bigoted or pornographic to sue the persons responsible.[57]

colorblindness. The ability, claimed by some liberals, to fail to notice—or, at least, ignore—the pigmentation of people's skins. To multiculturalists such as Adrienne Rich, this is "a form of naïveté and moral stupidity. It implies I would look at a black woman and see her as white, thus engaging in white solipsism to the utter erasure of her particular identity."[58] See also: **colordeafness; erasure; identity; white solipsism.**

colordeafness. A lack of talent, studied or real, for recognizing the difference between the speech patterns and modes of pronunciation of African-Americans and European-Americans, as, for example, being unable to distinguish between the accents of the Reverend Al Sharpton and George Plimpton.[59]

colorism. The prejudicial or preferential treatment of same-race people based solely on the color (e.g., the relative lightness or darkness) of their skin.[60]

communities of the African Diaspora. Ethnic groups dispersed from their historic African homeland by European and American slavers. It is appropriate to refer to members of such groups as **blacks of the African Diaspora** or **members of the African Diaspora.**[61]

companion. A gender-inclusive, nonheterosexist substitute for "boyfriend," "girlfriend," "wife," "husband," or "spouse." But because it is also a nonspeciesist substitute for "pet" or "animal friend," extreme care should be taken before using it.[62] Example: *"I now pronounce you companion and companion," intoned the liberation theologian.*

companion animal. See: animal companion.

compulsory heterosexuality. Poet-essayist Adrienne Rich defines this as "the enforcement of heterosexuality for women as a means of assuring male right of physical, economical, and emotional access." Also known as **coerced heterosexuality.**[63] See also: **heterosexual imperialism.**

condition. A sensitive and positive substitute for such melodramatic, and ultimately demeaning, phrases as "affliction," "malady," and "disease."[64] Example: *The Four Horse Oppressors of the Apocalypse were Nutritional Deprivation, State of Belligerency, Widespread Transmittable Condition, and Terminal Inconvenience.*

consensual nonmonogamy. Swapping sex partners.[65]

copper woman. Native American woman. This term became popular after the publication of *Daughters of Copper Woman,* a book written by Anne Cameron for the purpose of "preserving the fragile oral heritage" of West Coast indigenous peoples. The phrase seems to have fallen into disuse, however, perhaps as a consequence of what Canadian language reformer Betsy Warland describes as "a clearly stated directive" from Ms. Cameron's sister writers of color to "move over"—that is, "to desist from writing out of their cultures."[66]

cos. See: coself.

coself. Gender-neutral replacement for "herself" and "himself," recommended by feminist writer Mary Orovan. Example: *Wilma advised Charlie to go fuck* **coself**. Orovan also suggests that **co** be substituted for "she," "he," "him," and "her," and that the sexist possessive pronouns "his" and "her" be supplanted by **cos**.[67] (Note: Editors Cheris Kramarae and Paula A. Treichler of *A Feminist Dictionary* report the happy news that "co" is now being used in everyday speech by members of several alternative-life-style communities in Virginia and Missouri.[68])

cosmetically different. Ugly.[69] Example: Todd's favorite politically correct movie was *The Good, the Bad, and the* **Cosmetically Different**.

credentialism. Discriminating against a person by forcing her or him to provide evidence of ability, prior experience, knowledge, training, or the like, before being employed, admitted to an institution of learning, etc.[70]

crewed. One of the two adjectives officially designated by NASA as acceptable for use in place of the sexist term "manned" in describing space flights by human beings. Noted a NASA representative: "We have been ordered to delete any reference by sex, on the grounds that 'manned' flight is crude and 'crewed' is PC."[71] See also: **habitated**.

criminalized populations. Felons. The term is appropriate because it places the blame for illegal actions on the dominant culture and its institutions, rather than on the individual members of oppressed groups.[72]

cruelty-free products. Products that do not contain animal ingredients and are not tested on animals.[73] Example: *Despite the fact that her perfume was* **cruelty-free***, Lucinda was denied a seat in the discretionary-fragrance-free section of her favorite restaurant.*

cultural imperialism. The domination, marginalization or oppression of one culture by another.[74] Example: *Marga dismissed the media's lack of interest in her antipatriarchal lard sculpture as a typical manifestation of* **cultural imperialism**.

culturally dispossessed. A more accurate substitute for "culturally deprived." (Technically, *both* terms are incorrect because, as linguist Robert B. Moore explains, "third world children generally are bicultural, and many are bilingual, having grown up in their own culture as well as absorbing the dominant culture. In many ways they are equipped with skills and experiences which white youth have been deprived of, since most white youth develop in a monocultural, monolingual environment.").[75]

culturally sensitive. Politically correct. See: **multiculturalism**.

cultural tourism. Any attempt by a member of the dominant group to show an interest in, sample, or adopt the icons of a culture other than his or her own.[76] Example: *Marga dismissed the media's interest in her antipatriarchal lard sculpture as a typical manifestation of* **cultural tourism**.

cuntionary. See: **dicktion**.

custody suite. A more positive, less judgmental, term for what was once known as a "prison cell."[77]

D **date rape.** Acquaintance rape that occurs during a prearranged social engagement. Among the offenses specifically categorized as sexual assault in a landmark study on date rape conducted by Mary P. Koss of the University of Arizona is "intercourse as a result of intentionally getting the woman intoxicated." The Koss study found, perhaps not uncoincidentally, that 43 percent of the victims interviewed had not previously realized they had been raped.[78] Example: *After reading the Koss Report, the local chapter of Women Against* **Date Rape** *decided to change their slogan from "No means no!" to "Yes means no!"* See also: **acquaintance rape**.

decolonization. The act of freeing oneself from the bonds of one's oppressors.[79] See: **body decolonization**.

decon. An affectionate slang abbreviation for **deconstructionist** or **deconstructionism.**[80]

deconstructionism. A postmodern theory that, among other things, denies there is any objective definition of reality, posits that all literary works (i.e., "texts") are filled with self-contradictions and have no inherent meaning, and concludes, therefore, that no piece of writing is intrinsically more valuable than any other. Once one achieves even a superficial knowledge of deconstructionist analysis, one can easily understand the folly of insisting that the so-called "classics of Western literature"—works by Shakespeare, Homer, and Milton, for example—should be the core of any modern college literature curriculum.

deep ecology. See: biocentrism.

deficiency achievement. A nonjudgmental educational term meaning "failure."[81] Example: *At the graduation ceremony, Harry was given a special award for extraordinary* **deficiency** achievement.

dermatologically challenged. A terminal acne survivor, for example.[82]

developmentally challenged. Mentally retarded.[83] Also: **developmentally inconvenienced.**

diasporan, Diasporan. Of or pertaining to a **member of the African Diaspora.**[84]

Charlayne Hunter-Gault, a **diasporan** *anchor.*

dicktion. The style of writing and speech imposed upon the world by patriarchal white lexicographers. Hence, Betsy Warland, in her poem "the breasts refuse," refers to Noah Webster's **dicktionary**, and when Cheris Kramarae and Paula Treichler proposed the compilation of a *non*patriarchal lexicon, a linguistically alert anthropology student at the University of Sussex suggested they call it a **cuntionary**.[85]

dicktionary. See: dicktion.

differential framing. The sexist tendency of the television industry to focus on the faces of men and the bodies of women.[86] See also: **face-ism.**

An example of **differential framing.**

differently abled. Physically or mentally disabled. In the words of the Smith College Office of Student Affairs, the term was "created to underline the concept that differently abled individuals are just that, not less or inferior in any way [as the terms disabled, handicapped, etc. imply]."[87] Also: **differently able.**

differently advantaged. Poor.[88] Also: **economically exploited; economically marginalized.**

differently evolved. An adjective appropriate for describing a non-human animal, particularly one who has behaved in a manner upsetting to unenlightened human animals.[89] Example: *That shark isn't vicious. He/she just happens to be* **differently evolved.**

differently focused. Vague, spacey.[90]

differently hirsute. Bald.[91] Also: **follicularly challenged; hair disadvantaged.**

differently interesting. Boring.[92] Also: **charm-free.**

differently logical. Those whose reasoning powers are deemed inferior, and whose conclusions are therefore dismissed as "wrong," by the dominant logocentric majority.[93]

differently pleasured. Sado-masochistic.[94]

differently qualified. See: **uniquely proficient.**

differently sized. Obese.[95] See also: **alternative body image; horizontally challenged.**

difficult to serve. Nonjudgmental Canadian educators' term for "antisocial."[96] Example: *Mr. MacLaughlin was robbed at gunpoint by one of his* **difficult-to-serve** *students.*

discretionary fragrance. A foreign aromatic substance applied to the body, such as perfume, cologne, or after-shave lotion, so named because the individual wearing it has the discretion of not doing so. Since a person in the immediate vicinity of a user of such substances might be allergic to one or more oils or chemicals contained in them, it is increasingly considered politically incorrect to wear them. Indeed, the National Foundation for the Chemically Hypersensitive, of Marin County, California, insists that those wearing discretionary fragrances should be banned from public gathering places.[97] Example: *"Every woperson alive loves* **Discretionary Fragrance #5.** *"* See also: **nondiscretionary fragrance; scentism.**

diseasism. Discrimination against the ill by the temporarily healthy.

diseasist language. Language offensive to those who just happen to be unwell. Example: *"A cancer on the presidency"* and *"That's not funny, that's sick!"* *are two samples of patently* **diseasist** *language.*

diversity. Wide-ranging racial, ethnic, gender, and cultural representation. Reactionary opponents of multiculturalism are fond of saying that "diversity" is a synonym for "quotas."[98] If so, the term specifically excludes the policy of reserving space in American colleges for the otherwise unqualified sons and daughters of prominent European-American alumni.

domestic arts. A term, offered in Mary Ellen S. Capek's *A Woman's Thesaurus*, designed to give the field formerly known as "home economics" the respect patriarchal culture has always denied it.[99] Example: *In her* **domestic arts** *class, Betty learned how to use the casting techniques of Renaissance sculptors to make perfect Jell-O molds every time.* See also: **human ecology.**

domestic incarceration survivor. Housewife.[100]

A **domestic incarceration survivor.**

domestic partner. A live-in significant other; a spouse equivalent. In 1993, New York State made "domestic partnership" an officially recognized legal status. [101]

Woody Allen and Mia Farrow, an incompletely successful **domestic partnership.**

dominant culture. Mainstream.[102] Example: *As a result of the Supreme Court's controversial Brown decision of 1954, Ntzoke was required to attend a* **dominant culture** *school.*

DWEMs. Dead white European males, who were not only responsible for creating the vast majority of the irrelevant art, literature, and music that still form the core of the modern university curriculum, but also conspired to formulate the dominant patriarchal industrial order.[103]

Plato, a **dead white European male.**

E

ecodefender. See: ecowarrior.

ecofeminism. An activist movement based on the premise, in the words of Robin Morgan, that "degradation of the environment and degradation of female human beings go hand in fist."[104] "Even male supremacists sense the connection," Morgan explains. "More than one man has called a woman catty, a cow, bitch, bird, chick, vixen, shrew, tomato, lemon—spitting contempt for women and for the natural world in the same pejorative slang that speaks of raping virgin forests."[105]

economically exploited. Poor. The term "economically disadvantaged," once considered a paragon of sensitivity, is no longer acceptable, Robert B. Moore explains in "Racial Stereotyping in the English Language," because it "blames the victim"; i.e., it "places responsibility of poverty on the victims of poverty." "Economically exploited," however, puts the blame where it belongs—"on those in power who benefit from, and continue to permit, poverty."[106]

economically marginalized. Poor. A term, first used by *Christianity Today*, which some liberals find useful because it is slightly less hard on "oppressors" than "economically exploited."[107]

ecotage. Sabotage to prevent the corporate rape of the environment. Two examples of ecotage are **tree-spiking**, the studding of trees with large nails to prevent sawing, and **monkeywrenching**, the "decommissioning"—that is, the destruction—of earth-moving machinery.[108] See also: **ecowarrior.**

ecoterrorist. See: ecowarrior.

ecoteur. See: ecowarrior.

ecowarrior. An individual who engages in ecotage in an attempt to save the environment. It is also appropriate to call ecowarriors "ecodefenders" or "ecoteurs"—but *not* "ecoterrorists." "The monkeywrencher must very carefully weigh the possibility of harm to any person from ecotage," Earth First! cofounder Dave Foreman explains, "and must act to insure that no humans are hurt. *Ecodefense* constantly underscores this point and offers many safety suggestions—including the need for large, clear warnings about spiked trees....The true ecoterrorists are the planet-despoilers."[109] See: ecotage.

efemcipated. Emancipated, especially as it applies to the liberation and empowerment of women. The term was introduced by Bina Goldfield, who used it in the title of *The Efemcipated English Handbook,* a volume "designed to guide you to the use of an alternative language and perhaps inspire you to carry it to as yet undreamed of possibilities."[110] See: **wofem.**

ego-testicle worldview. The social critic Adelaida R. Del Castillo defines this handy term as "men's point of view on all issues."[111]

electorally slighted. An appropriately nonjudgmental term for a losing political candidate.[112]

George Bush, an **electorally slighted** *presidential candidate.*

emergent. An adjective denoting a member of one or more under-represented identity groups. Example: *Cherríe Moraga, coeditor of* This Bridge Called My Back: Writings by Radical Women of Color, *is Todd's favorite* **emergent** *poet-anthologist.*

emotionally different. Psychologically disturbed; crazy.[113]

enclosure. The act of sexual intercourse, redefined as a gender-fair substitute for such phallocentric concepts as "penetration" and "insertion."[114] Example: **Enclose** *yourself and the horse you oppressed by riding in on!* Also: **engulfment.**[115]

engulfment. See: **enclosure.**

enslaved person. The correct word for "slave"—a term which is culturally insensitive because it ignores the essential humanity of those enslaved.[116]

environmental hygienist. Janitor.[117]

environmental racism. The siting of smokestacks, sewage treatment centers, etc., in predominantly African-American or Latino neighborhoods.[118]

epicene. Capable of referring to either sex.[119] Example: *The word "coself," coined to replace "himself" and "herself," is an* **epicene** *pronoun.* See also: **ambigenic.**

erasure. The marginalization of a racial, gender, cultural, or political group to the point where it becomes so powerless that it is, for all practical purposes, invisible to the mainstream of society.[120] Example: *Gloria refused to kiss Brad on the grounds that doing so would be a self-inflicted contribution to the* **erasure** *of her gender.*

ethically disoriented. Dishonest.[121] Example: *"Hands up or I'll plug ya!" cried the* **ethically disoriented**—*and blatantly ableist*—*bank robber.* See also: **morally different.**

ethnocentrism. Defined by the Smith College Office of Student Affairs as "oppression of cultures other than the dominant one in the belief that the dominant way of doing things is the superior way."[122]

Euro-American worldview. Florida A&M professors Yvonne R. Bell, Cathy L. Bouie, and Joseph A. Baldwin, writing in the *Journal of Black Studies*, define a "Euro-American worldview" based on the basic principles of "survival of the fittest" and "control over nature" (people, objects, material possessions). "Mastery," they add "is achieved through competition, aggression, materialism, domination and power, oppression, independence, and the transformation and rearranging of objects in nature."[123] For Ms. Bell's, Ms. Bouie's, and Mr. Baldwin's definition of the African-American worldview, see **African-American worldview.**

Eurocentric/cultural deprivation framework. The systematic denial by America's white power elite of the validity—or, indeed, the right to exist—of any "American" culture other than their own European-based one.[124]

Eurocentrism. The view that Europe was the focal point of human history, and that, as a result, white-male-heterosexual-dominated "Western" culture is somehow superior to all other ways of life and deserves to hold a privileged place in society.[125] See also: **Afrocentrism.**

European-influenced African-American. An African-American who exhibits behavior that would be considered racist if it weren't impossible, by definition, for members of groups without an institutional power base to engage in racism. The term was coined at the University of Cincinnati to describe a student of color who shouted "Arab go home!" during a pro–Persian Gulf War rally.[126] See: **institutional power; oppression.**

exceptional. Mentally retarded or physically disabled. Although use of this term is generally deemed appropriate, **mentally challenged, physically challenged,** and **differently abled** are considered by many to present people with disabilities in a more "positive" light.[127]

expediting students' progress toward alternate life pursuits. An innovatively sensitive term for "expelling, kicking out, or dismissing students," coined by the administrators of Wright State University in Dayton, Ohio.[128]

experientially enhanced.   Old.[129] See also: **mature; seasoned; senior; chronologically gifted; longer-living.**

F **face-ism.**   The oppressive tendency of the dominant culture media to present pictures of men from the neck up only, but to show the entire bodies of women.[130] Example: *"If television isn't face-ist,"* asked Astrid, *"why haven't I ever seen Dan Rather's calves?"* See also: **differential framing.**

false consciousness.   The failure of even the most well-intentioned members of empowered groups to see that their arguments and beliefs are the products of an oppressive social system, and are therefore irrelevant, useless, and totally meaningless.[131] False consciousness can also victimize individuals in marginalized groups, who sometimes become so seduced by the dominant culture's propaganda that they fail to realize that they have been oppressed; this "false consciousness of the underrepresented" is often called **internalized oppression.** See also: **intellectual indenture.**

familism.   Sociologist Margrit Eichler defines this as a specific form of age-, race-, or gender-insensitivity in which an action or experience "is attributed to a family or household when in fact the action is carried out, or the event potentially differentially experienced, by individuals within the unit." Familism can lead, Eichler warns, to such distortions as the question "What do you think your parents would like you to do when you leave school?" which presupposes that the mother and father agree on this issue, or the assumption that household income is "necessarily of equal benefit" to all family members, "irrespective of who controls it."[132] Example: *It was very* **familist** *of Vito to assume that all the Colombos wanted him iced, just because the Don, "Horizontally Challenged" Vinnie, had put out a contract on him.*

fatism. Discrimination against people of size by the hegemonic nonfat majority.[133] "Since there is evidence that being fat is related to one's racial or class origins," writes Martha Courtot in *A Spoiled Identity*, "this is one more way the system acts to grind down the poor."[134] See also: **sizeism; weightism.**

fatophobia. The conviction that all animals, including human ones, come in a "standard size," and that, consequently, obesity is unnatural and wrong.[135]

Oprah Winfrey, an intermittently **fatophobic** *individual.*

feelism. Bias in favor of fuzzy, furry, or cuddly organisms over ones that are slimy and clammy.[136] Example: *Jason's preference for the rabbit over the snake at the petting wildlife preservation center revealed his* **feelist** *prejudices.*

feline-American. A cat who resides in the United States.[137]

femhole. A replacement for the word "manhole," coined by Bina Goldfield, author of *The Efemcipated English Handbook,* to dramatize the linguistic and cultural erasure of women in the electrical and sanitation trades.[138] See also: **maintenance hatch; personhole; personnel access structure; utility hole.**

A **femhole.**

femmchismo. A nonphallocentric gender attitude characterized by active rather than passive behavior on the part of the female sexual partner.[139]

femstruate. A term suggested by Bina Goldfield, who defines it as "to discharge the femses."[140]

femtal. A neologism coined by Bina Goldfield to celebrate the innate mental ability of women.[141]

ferms. A term coined by Brown University geneticist Anne Fausto-Sterling to describe members of one of at least three sexes she identifies as lying between "female" and "male" on the gender spectrum. Ferms possess ovaries and some aspects of the male genitalia, but they do not have testes.[142] See also: **herms** and **merms.**

first baseperson. The correct gender-inclusive term for "first baseman," recommended by officials of the Little League after its national program became coeducational.[143]

flesh. Meat. "Why not use accurate language?" asks *The Washington Post* columnist Colman McCarthy. "Such words as meat, beef, pork, veal, or poultry are the Adolph's tenderizers of language: They make gruesomeness palatable." Another synonym for "meat" suggested by McCarthy is **scorched corpses of animals**, a phrase originally coined by George Bernard Shaw.[144] See also: **processed animal carcasses.**

floral companion. See: **botanical companion.**

follicularly challenged. Bald.[145] Also: **differently hirsute; hair disadvantaged.**

fortuitarianism. The belief that, since humans have no right to interfere with the natural life cycle of a member of any other species, they should eat only meat from animals that have died accidentally (those that have been run over by trucks, for example) and fruits and vegetables that have become separated from their parent plant either through the action of gravity or some other natural event, such as wind or the process of ripening.[146]

foundationalism. The doctrine that inquiry or thought can actually be grounded on pregiven principles that are true beyond mere belief or assumption. Postmodern analysis shows us that no such principles or truths exist, and that any attempt to establish or prove that they do is merely an exercise in "self-constituted logic."[147] Example: *The statement "We hold these truths to be self-evident" is blatantly—and pathetically—foundationalist.*

fragrance-free zones. See: **scentism**.

free-roaming. Nonspeciesist term for "wild."[148] Example: *Sarah was mauled by a free-roaming boar.*

freshpeople. First-year students. It is also acceptable to call freshpeople **freshpersons** or **frosh**.[149]

fruitarian. An individual who, for ethical and/or health reasons, declines to eat anything whose gathering or processing is impossible without the killing of animals or plants. Some fruitarians favor a diet of fruit, seeds, nuts, honey, and olive oil; others, who also adhere to the tenets of the veganism movement, forswear the honey on the grounds that it is a stolen nonhuman animal product.[150] See also: **vegan; stolen products**.

fumerist. Kate Clinton's term for the idealized feminist humorist—"a sparkling incendiary with blazes of light and insight" who would deliver "whys-cracks," not wisecracks. According to Naomi Weisstein, fumerists should display a "humor which recognizes a common oppression, notices its source and the roles it requires, [and] identifies the agents of oppression." But, try as she might, Weisstein complains in her article "Why We Aren't Laughing Anymore" that she's been unable to find anything that meets her definition.[151] Example: *"I can't hear you—I am aurally inconvenienced as a result of having a fructal companion in my ear,"* quipped the **fumerist**.

G **gay.** The preferred term for a male homosexual. However, a self-described "spokeslesbian" for the advocacy group Queer Nation has demanded that the term "queer" be used instead. "Gay," journalist Mat Coward quotes her as saying, refers to "a certain kind of white, middle-class assimilationist." "No doubt this will all seem vital news to homosexual Kurds, starving on Mt. Ignatieff," Coward observes.[152]

gender advisor. A counselor who would help intersexuals decide whether to maintain their natural positions on the female-male continuum, or to enlist the aid of what geneticist Anne Fausto-Sterling calls "a surgical shoehorn" in an effort to become "normal" males or females.[153] See: **ferms, herms, intersexual, merms,** and **two-party sexual system.**

gender-enders. A term used by the Multicultural Management Program Fellows [sic] of the University of Missouri Journalism School to describe sex-marked suffixes such as "-ess" (as in "waitress"), "-enne" (as in "comedienne"), "-ix" (as in "aviatrix"), and "-ette" (as in "majorette").[154] As nonsexist language specialists Casey Miller and Kate Swift have pointed out, feminine "gender-enders" imply that the male is the norm and the female the aberration.[155] Therefore, all words employing such suffixes must be avoided.

gender-neutral. Nonableist improvement upon "gender-blind."[156]

generously cut. Nonsizeist substitute for "extra-large."[157] See also: **size-friendly.**

genetically oppressive. White.[158]

Albert Schweitzer, a **genetically oppressive** *person.*

gingerbread person. Desexualized replacement for "gingerbread man."[159] Example: *"It's raining nonhuman companion animals,"* said Wendy and Melissa's father. *"Why don't you prewomen have an herbal tea party for your nonsexist dolls, and then we'll bake some* **gingerbread persons***!"* Also: **gingerbread figure**.

gradualism. A willingness, on the part of less-than-fully-committed advocates of change, to work within the existing system—to "settle," as biocentrist Dave Macauley phrases it, "for a kind of reformism…that fails to challenge the roots of our contemporary malaise."[160]

grammar. Defined by Lewis Lapham as "arbitrary rules of literary procedure subservient to a sexist political agenda."[161] Example: *"Being as* **grammar** *is nothing but an ethnocentric white patriarchal reconstruction of language,"* read the memo from the English Department, *"hopefully we can eradicate it in no uncertain terms from and in regard to the curriculum at present."*

guest. Patient; inmate; prisoner.[162] See also: **client of the correctional system**.

gynocentric be-ing. Lesbianism.[163] See also: **women-identified women**.

gynophobia. The fear and hatred of women.[164]

H

Ha. Abbreviation for "Human animal"—a nonspeciesist, non-gender-specific substitute for the titles "Ms." and "Mr." proposed by the American Hyphen Society. Nonhuman animals would be addressed as **Nha**. See: **human animal; Pn**.

habitated. One of two gender-inclusive terms adopted by NASA to replace the sexist adjective "manned" in describing space flights involving the participation of human crewmembers.[165] See also: **crewed**.

hair disadvantaged. *The Japan Economic Journal*'s term for "bald," rapidly gaining currency in the U.S.[166] See also: **differently hirsute; follicularly challenged.**

Mikhail S. Gorbachev, a **hair disadvantaged** *individual.*

hand-held American. A puppet designed, built or manipulated by a person born or residing in the United States.[167]

handi-capable. Gifted with a physical disability.[168] Similar coinages endorsed by the American Hyphen Society include: "spas-tickety-boo"; "HIV-positively wonderful"; "stutterrific" (for a person who stutters); "squintessentially great" (for an individual who squints) and, for the brain-dead or permanently comatose, "veget-able."

have (a condition, disability, or disease). See: **with.**

hegemony. The domination exercised by mainstream groups over all those possessing differing racial, ethnic, national, creedal, gender, or sexual identities.[169]

heightism. Discrimination against the vertically challenged.[170]

Heightism *survivors Abomah the African Giantess and friend, ca. 1920.*

hera. A female hero. The term not only avoids the male connotations of the word "hero" and the trivializing of women inherent in the process of adding the suffix "-ine" to "hero" to create "heroine," but also evokes the grandeur and power of the ancient goddess Hera.[171] See also: **she-ro.**

herms. Brown University professor Anne Fausto-Sterling uses this term to describe individuals whom dominant culture medical professionals call "true hermaphrodites"—intersexuals having one ovary and one testis. According to Fausto-Sterling, division of the human race into only two genders is an artificial construction of Western culture; herms are one of at least five sexes that lie along the female-to-male continuum.[172] See also: **ferms** and **merms.**

herstory. The *Random House Webster's College Dictionary* defines this as "History (used as an alternative form to distinguish or emphasize the particular experience of women)."[173] *A Woman's New World Dictionary* amplifies this as "1. The past as seen through the eyes of women. 2. The removal of male self-glorification from history."[174] However, Mary Daly, who teaches feminist ethics in the Department of Theology of Boston College, finds the term "herstory" unacceptable, since it implies that the achievements of women constitute a separate, minor branch of the story of personkind. See also: **hystery.**

heterocentrism. The belief that heterosexuality is somehow superior to, or more "natural" and "normal" than, homosexuality or lesbianism.

heterosexism. "Oppression of those of sexual orientations other than heterosexual, such as gays, lesbians and bisexuals; this can take place by not acknowledging their existence" (as defined by the Smith College Office of Student Affairs).[175]

heterosexual imperialism. The patriarchal domination of women through "coerced heterosexuality," which, in the words of diasporan poet Cheryl Clarke, "manifests itself in the family, the state, and Madison Avenue." "Women are kept, maintained, and contained," Clarke observes, "through terror, violence and spray of semen."[176] See also: **compulsory heterosexuality**.

heterosexually celibate. Frigid. Dr. Dale Spender points out that the patriarchal term "frigidity" fails to take into account the possibility that a woman's refusal to participate in sexual intercourse "could be a form of power against an oppressor."[177]

himmicane. Substitute for "hurricane," coined to protest patriarchal male weatherpeople's insistence on naming destructive tropical storms after women. As Francine Wattman Frank and Paula A. Treichler point out in *Language, Gender, and Professional Writing*, the feminist argument succeeded in bringing about change—the storms are now given alternate male and female names.[178]

his 'n' herstory. History. (A gender-inclusive term suggested by columnist Peter Leo.)[179]

hispes survivor. A man with herpes. (A term suggested by columnist Peter Leo.)[180]

homophobia. Defined by the Smith College Office of Student Affairs as "the fear of gays, lesbians, and bisexuals." But, because "homo" in Latin means not only "same," but also "man," many feminists insist that **lesbophobia** is the only correct term for unreasoning fear of, or antipathy toward, women-identified women.[181]

horizontally challenged. Fat. See also: **alternative body image; differently sized**.

h'orsh'it. An artful contraction of "he or she or it," offered by Joel Forbes in 1975 as a gender-free pronoun.[182]

houseless. A more sensitive term for "homeless," coined by a Long Island schoolteacher who informed a group of local street people they were "houseless but not homeless, because home is wherever you are."[183] See also: **involuntarily undomiciled; underhoused**.

hufem. A substitute for the word "human," coined by Bina Gold-field, author of *The Efemcipated English Handbook*,[184] and particularly useful as a means of reminding men that they represent slightly less than 50 percent of personkind.

human animal. Nonspeciesist substitute for the anthropocentric "human."[185]

Dag Hammarskjöld, a **human animal.**

human companion of a nonhuman companion. The American Humane Society's new non-speciesist, gender-neutral term for the "owner" or "master" of what used to be called a "pet."[186]

human difference. A more nurturing substitute for the word "disability," advocated by members of the aurally-inconvenienced community to counter the negative images which an ableist society automatically associates with persons described as "disabled."[187]

human ecology. What used to be called "home economics" until the University of Texas changed the name of its "Department of Home Economics" to the "Department of Human Ecology."[188] Example: *In her* **human ecology** *course, Maria learned how to apply the same forces of hydraulic ablation that shaped the Grand Canyon to the task of removing stubborn stains from garments and utensils.* See also: **domestic arts.**

human resources. Nonsexist replacement for "manpower."[189]

humanslaughter. See: personslaughter.

humantarian (not to be confused with "humanitarian"). A nonjudgmental term for a cannibal.[190]

Hannibal Lecter, a noted **humantarian.**

humyn. Even-handedly nonsexist replacement for the phallogeneric "human."[191]

hung punct. The deconstructionist technique of extending a punctuation mark that occurs at the end of a line of text into the margin to symbolize a concern for the marginalization of people and ideas.[192]

hygienism. The belief that personal cleanliness can be an indicator of a person's value; a deep-seated cultural bias in favor of the opinion that dirt and grime are somehow unhealthy, wrong, or bad.[193] Example: *Benjamin's mother betrayed both* **hygienist** *and* speciesist *attitudes when she stated that his room was "as filthy as a pigsty."*

hystery. History, especially as it reflects the accomplishments and perspective of women. *The Flame* magazine, which coined the word, feels "hystery" is superior to the more widely used **herstory** because it "emphasizes origin or womb."[194]

ice people. The European-American descendants of northern Ice Age peoples. The term was coined by Dr. Leonard Jeffries, chairman [sic] of the Afro-American Studies Department of the City University of New York, who theorizes that humanity is divided into two principal groups, "ice people" and "sun people" (Africans, Asians, and natives of Latin America and the Caribbean). The two groups have diametrically opposed value systems: ice people are materialistic, egotistical, and exploitive, while sun people are humanistic, communal, and caring.[195] See also: **snow person.**

Mother Teresa, an **ice person.**

ice person. See: ice people.

iceperson. Nonsexist substitute for "iceman." Not to be confused with an **ice person.** The U.S. Department of Labor, in its snappily named *Job Title Revisions to Eliminate Sex- and Age-Referent Language from the Dictionary of Occupational Titles,* also recommends **ice route driver.**[196]

ichthyo-American. A fish who resides in the territorial or inland waters of the United States.[197]

identity. The race, gender, ethnicity, geographic origin, language, nationality, culture, socioeconomic class, sexual preference, lifestyle, religion, size, body type, age, worldview, abilities, and/or experiences by which persons or groups define themselves or are defined.[198]

identity group.   A group of people who share a common identity.[199]

identity politics.   See: politics of difference.

illegal alien.   An appropriate phrase, Amoja Three Rivers points out in *Cultural Etiquette: A Guide for the Well-Intentioned*, for use in referring to the descendents of the Europeans who illegally seized the "North American continent" (Turtle Island) in the first place. The term is offensive, however, when applied to undocumented workers, especially Latinas and Latinos who enter the U.S. along the illegal border created in 1848 when the so-called "American Southwest" was stolen from Mexico.[200] See also: **Turtle Island.**

in an orderly transition between career changes.   Unemployed.[201] See also: **indefinitely idled; involuntarily leisured; nonwaged; occupationally dispossessed; vocationally deprived.**

inclusive.   Including or embracing everyone who should be included or embraced; nonoppressive; culturally sensitive; politically correct.[202]

incomplete success.   Failure. The term was originally coined in 1980 by President Jimmy Carter to characterize the raid to free the American hostages in Iran.[203]

inconvenienced.   A positive synonym for "disabled," coined to emphasize the fact that people's disabilities need not prevent them from being **handi-capable.**[204]

increasingly distracted. Senile.[205]

indefinitely idled. Unemployed.[206] See also: **in an orderly transition between career changes; involuntarily leisured; nonwaged; occupationally dispossessed; vocationally deprived.**

indigenous peoples.   A preferred name for racial or ethnic groups who lived in the Western Hemisphere before the Eurocentrics arrived. "Native peoples" is also widely considered appropriate, although the use of the word "native" in such derogatory imperialist phrases as "the natives are restless" may render it offensive to some. "Native Americans," once the term of choice, has fallen from favor because the word "American," derived from the name of Italian adventurer Amerigo Vespucci, is European in origin. Some members of indigenous groups suggest that they still wish to be called American Indians (indeed, the most prominent indigenous people's rights organization is called the "American Indian Movement"). This is a request that must be respected, even if, as some multiculturalists have argued, those who make it are unconsciously contributing to their own oppression. Probably the best solution—all the more so because it acknowledges the diversity of the indigenous population—is to use the name of the specific nation (e.g., Cherokee, Iroquois, Navajo) that an individual represents. Finally, a word of warning from Amylee, director of the Native American Indian Resource Center and author of "How Not to Talk to an Indian": "Amerind" and "Amerindian" are "anthropologists' labels." "Considering the source," she adds, these terms are "offensive—used by a pseudo-intellectual clique." [207] See also: **Native American.**

individual with temporarily unmet objectives. A ne'er-do-well; a loser; a failure.

inning. See: outing.

insignificant other. An ex-wife, ex-husband, ex-boyfriend or ex-girlfriend.[208]

institutional power. Access to political, economic, and interpersonal resources (such as networking or social acceptance) within the dominant culture and its institutions.[209]

intellectual indenture. The adherence by a critic or professor of color to European or European-American literary theories or standards.[210] Example: *Denise's love of Renaissance poetry revealed a degree of* **intellectual indenture** *that called into question the advisability of her continuing to serve on the faculty.* See also: **false consciousness.**

internalized oppression. Any of several forms of false consciousness that lead members of unempowered groups to accept or actively support their own victimization. One extreme manifestation of internalized oppression is the tendency of some exploited individuals to identify with—and even come to feel they love—their oppressors.[211] See: **false consciousness.**

intersexual. A member of one of at least three genders that lie between "male" and "female" on the human sexual continuum. The notion that there are only two sexes is merely a construction of Western culture, which, in the words of Brown University medical science professor Anne Fausto-Sterling, is "committed" to "maintaining a two-party sexual system" because intersexual bodies "challenge traditional beliefs about sexual difference."[212] See: **two-party sexual system.**

interspecies communicator. A nonhuman-animal trainer.[213]

An **interspecies communicator.**

Inuit. The correct term for a Canadian of what used to be called "Eskimo" descent. The word "Eskimo" is considered offensive, at least in part because the Inuits long believed, erroneously, that it meant "eater of raw meat."[214] See also: **Native Alaskan.**

Inupat. See: **Native Alaskan.**

invisible. A term denoting an individual or group so unempowered that her, his, or its existence is scarcely noted in the day-to-day language, culture, and rituals of the mainstream.[215]

involuntarily leisured. Unemployed.[216] See also: **in an orderly transition between career changes; indefinitely idled; nonwaged; occupationally dispossessed; vocationally deprived.**

involuntarily undomiciled. Homeless.[217] See also: **houseless; underhoused.**

involved. Severely crippled.[218]

ismizationism. See: anti-ismizationism.

J **Jewish person.** The preferred term for use in referring to followers of Judaism or people of Jewish descent. The word "Jew," the University of Missouri Journalism School's Multicultural Management Program tells us, is found "offensive" by some and should probably be avoided.[219]

just happens to be. Is (especially when identifying a member of an oppressed group). However, as the noted Afrocentrist Molefi Kete Asante points out, for an African-American to say he or she "just happens to be black" is an inexcusable act of self-denial.[220]

Adolf Hitler, who **just happened to be** *the murderer of 6,000,000 Jewish persons.*

K **kingdomism.** Discrimination against flora or minerals by fauna.[221] Example: *It was* **kingdomistic** *of Herman to advocate the shunning of animal products while condoning a diet of vegetables and fruit.* (Note: Since "kingdom" is itself a phallogeneric term, the Hyphen

The lima bean, a victim of **kingdomism.**

Society suggests **realmism** [as in the vegetable, mineral, and animal realms].)

knowledge-base nonpossessor. A person, especially a student, who knows absolutely nothing about a given subject; an ignoramus.[222]

Kwanzaa. A harvest festival observed from December 26 to January 1 as an Afrocentric alternative to Christmas and Chanukah.[223] It is widely assumed that Kwanzaa is an ancient African tradition, but the first Kwanzaa was actually celebrated in Los Angeles in 1966.

Lacto-ovo-vegetarianism. A revisionist offshoot of the vegetarian movement, condemned by strict animal rights activists, which permits the ingestion of dairy products and eggs.[224] See: **vegan.**

language castration. The "cutting away" of the "phallus-centered value system imposed by patriarchy, in its subtle as well as its more manifest expressions." (As called for by Mary Daly in "Theology After the Demise of God the Father: A Call for the Castration of Sexist Religion."[225])

larger-than-average citizen. One who might once have been characterized as fat.[226] Also: **person of size; person of substance.**

Latino/Latina. Names self-created by those of Latin-American descent and culture to emphasize their connection with that part of the world.[227] According to *The New York Times*, "Latino" and "Latina" are considered more appropriate than "Hispanic," since the latter term was, to a large degree, "imposed" by the U.S. Census Department. Says author Sandra Cisneros, who refuses to permit her work to appear in any anthology that contains the word "Hispanic": "It's a repulsive slave name."[228]

least best. Worst. A term used by the United Parcel Service in evaluating its drivers.[229]

lesbophobia. The fear or hatred of lesbians. The term is preferable to "homophobia" when used in reference to women, since "homophobia" contains the prefix "homo," which, because it can mean "man" as well as "same," is regarded by some as phallogeneric.[230]

linguistic purism. The doctrine stating that any reforms aimed at excising demeaning usage and terminology from the English language should be resisted in the name of preserving the integrity of what is hypocritically called "the mother tongue." "Language is not static but dynamic," protests Felicia Mitchell of Emory & Henry College, "and other linguistic changes have been wrought with much less ado....It is not the purity of the language [traditionalists] are worrying about. It is the sanctity of a male-dominated language."[231] See also: **anti-ismizationism.**

lit crit. An affectionate—and favored—term for postmodernist literary criticism. According to Professor Thomas McLaughlin of Appalachian State University, the theories underlying lit crit—deconstructionism, semiotics, and reader-response criticism, to name just a few—have "permeated our thinking" to the point where they have "defined for our times how discourse about literature, as well as culture in general, shall proceed."[232] Two of the prime tenets of lit crit are that no text has intrinsic value and that the reader is far more important than the writer. It is not hard to see, therefore, why Yale professor Geoffrey Hartman argues that "works of commentary" must now be valued as much, if not more, than "works of art."[233] From among the flurry of such "works of commentary" that lit crit has produced, the American Hyphen Society particularly recommends "Jane Austen and the Masturbating Girl," by Duke University English professor Eve Sedgwick.[234]

logocentrism. The belief—in the face of evidence to the contrary presented by deconstructionist Jacques Derrida—that truth, meaning, and reality are actually "knowable" and can thus be represented by language, and that those claiming "knowledge" or the ability to use words clearly or argue convincingly are thus somehow superior to those who cannot. Logocentrism is commonly accompanied by a feeling of contempt for the differently logical.[235]

longer-living, the. The elderly. The term became popular after Mario Cuomo, running for office in New York State, suggested that the Department of Aging be renamed the "Department of Longer Living."[236] See also: **mature; seasoned; senior; chronologically gifted; experientially enhanced.**

lookism. "The belief that appearance is an indicator of a person's value; the construction of a standard for beauty/attractiveness; and oppression through stereotypes and generalizations of both those who do not fit that standard and those who do" (as defined by the Smith College Office of Student Affairs).[237] Example: *"You are a much more likely victim of look-ism without your glasses on, Ms. Kinsley," leered the professor.*

Brigitte Bardot, a **lookism** *survivor.*

M **maintenance hatch.** A gender-neutral substitute for "manhole."[238] See also: **femhole; personhole; personnel access structure; utility hole.**

A **maintenance hatch.**

male motherhood. Mary Daly offers this useful definition: "1. fundamental reversal characteristic of patriarchal myth, e.g. god the father creating the world, Adam giving birth to Eve, Zeus bringing forth Athena. 2. male attempts to possess the creative powers of women, resulting in berserk and destructive simulations of motherhood—exemplified in the activities of obstetricians and gynecologists. 3. male endeavors to self-generate by means of necrological reproductive technologies which reduce females to the conditions of incubators/vessels and which are inherently directed toward the annihilation of women."[239]

malestream. Defined in *A Feminist Dictionary* as designating "that body of thought judged by *(white educated) males* to constitute the mainstream."[240]

malism. The antithesis of feminism.[241] Example: *In her book* Feminist Versus Malist Sexual Political Philosophy, *Mia Albright postulates an ideal world in which our "Judaic-Christian malist society" would be transcended by a feminist one.* Also known as **masculism.**[242]

Manglish. Feminist Varda One's term for "the English language as it is used by men in the perpetuation of male supremacy." [243]

marginalize. To place or force into a position of marginal importance, influence or power.[244]

masculism. See: malism.

mature. Old. See also: senior; seasoned; longer-living; chronologically gifted; experientially enhanced.

mechanical-American. A robot manufactured, or employed, in the United States or its territories.[245]

melanin impoverished. White.[246] The term was inspired by Professor Leonard Jeffries of the City College of New York, who has written that "white folks are deficient in melanin" and thus are "less biologically proficient" than blacks.[247] Example: *Todd's favorite politically correct fairy tale was "Snow* **Melanin-Impoverished** *and the Seven Vertically Challenged Individuals."*

Louis XIV,
a **melanin-impoverished** person.

member of a career-offender cartel. An ethnically unexceptionable substitute for "mafioso," courtesy of the New Jersey State Crime Control Commission.[248]

member of the African Diaspora. An African-American or Caribbean-American, for example. Also: **black of the African Diaspora.**[249] See: **communities of the African Diaspora.**

member of the mutant albino genetic-recessive global minority. A white person.[250] See: **mutant albino genetic-recessive global minority.**

mental activity at the margin. Kate Millett's more sensitive term for what used to be called "insanity."[251]

mentally challenged. A more sensitive substitute for the demeaning phrase "mentally retarded." Also an appropriate synonym for "stupid."[252] See also: **cerebrally challenged.**

merms. Individuals possessing testes and some aspects of female genitalia, but who have no ovaries. The term was coined by Anne Fausto-Sterling, a geneticist and intersexual rights advocate who teaches at Brown University. According to Fausto-Sterling, there are at least two genders besides females, males and merms, and there may indeed be many more.[253] See also: **ferms** and **herms.**

metabolically different. The Berkeley Rhetoric Department's suggested replacement for "dead."[254] See also: **terminally inconvenienced.**

mineral companion. Nonkingdomist term for "pet rock."[255]

A boy and his **mineral companion.**

misogyny. Hatred of, or hostility toward, women.[256]

misorientation. The misguided belief, held by certain members of unempowered groups, that they share the same history as the dominant culture.[257]

mister-ectomy. Mary Daly of the Boston College Department of Theology defines this as the most foolproof way for women "to get off the hook of the heterosexually defined contraceptive dilemma."[258]

monkeywrenching. See: ecotage.

monocultural. Of or pertaining to a single cultural group (especially the white male heterosexual patriarchal Eurocentric culture that dominates American society); nonmulticultural.[259]

morally different. Dishonest; immoral; evil.[260] See also: **ethically disoriented.**

Pol Pot, a **morally different** *person.*

motivationally deficient. Lazy. Because the word "deficient" has the quality of "blaming the victim" for a condition more properly attributed to the failures of society, this phrase is more and more frequently being replaced by the less judgmental **motivationally dispossessed.**[261]

motivationally dispossessed. Lazy.[262] Example: *Todd's favorite politically correct song was "Roll Out Those* **Motivationally Dispossessed,** *Visibility-Reduced, Emotionally Challenged Days of Summer."* See also: **motivationally deficient.**

msterbation. Female auto-eroticism. See also: **mstrful.**

msterful. A nonpatriarchal term for "authoritative, self-willed, imperious."[263] See also: **msterbation.**

multicult. Postmodernist slang for "multicultural" or **multiculturalism.**[264]

multiculti. Proponents of the multiculturalism movement.[265]

multiculturalism. A broad, pluralistic social movement that, through the celebration of "difference," champions a more tolerant, diverse, inclusive, and realistic view of America and (in the memorable words of the New York State Social Studies Review and Development Committee) "the peoples who person it."[266] Indeed, "multiculturalism" encompasses virtually the entire spectrum of views that have come to be known, not always without irony, as "politically correct." Unfortunately, since reactionary critics have co-opted the term in a none-too-subtle attempt to silence the **multiculti,** it is no longer "politically correct" to say "politically correct." (American Hyphen Society researchers discovered this fact too late to have the offending words excised from the title of this book—an error for which we are deeply apologetic.)

mutant albino genetic-recessive global minority. White people. This term is particularly useful in dramatizing the point that melanin impoverishment is a biological sport—a mutation—that would have quickly evolved out of existence had white male supremacists not conspired to prevent free sexual relations between their race and those whom Frances Cress Welsing, a noted Washington, D.C., psychiatrist and Afrocentrist, calls "skin-color genetically-dominant black, brown, red, and yellow peoples."[267] It is appropriate to refer to individual members of the white race as **members of the mutant albino genetic-recessive global minority.** See also: **skin-color genetically dominant world majority.**

muted group. An identity group subordinated to the point where its voice carries little weight with those in the dominant culture. Because of its ableist connotations, this term, once common, has fallen into general disuse.[268] See also: **marginalize.**

N **Native Alaskan.** A preferred term for what used to be called the "Eskimo" peoples of Alaska and the Aleutian Islands. Unlike the Inuits of Canada, some Native Alaskans reportedly do not mind being called "Eskimos," but the American Hyphen Society feels this is merely a manifestation of false consciousness and strongly advises readers to shun the term. Also permissible are **Alaskan native** and **indigenous Alaskan;** but the most "correct" usage of all is to call Native Alaskan groups by their specific ethnic names, e.g. the **Aleuts,** the **Inupats,** and the **Yupiks.**[269] See: **false consciousness.**

Native American. American Indian. See: **indigenous peoples.**

needs assessment. The preferred term for "educational testing." "Testing" is unacceptable because it places the responsibility for "shortcomings" on the student, ignoring the far more significant contribution of the educational system and, indeed, of society.[270] Example: *"Darn! I got a grade of "differently superior" on my final needs assessment," sobbed Naomi.*

negative attention getting. Misbehavior.[271] Example: *Todd's favorite politically correct jazz composition was Thomas "Differ-*

ently Sized" Waller's "Ain't Engagin' in **Negative Attention Gettin'."**

negative saver. Nonjudgmental synonym for "spendthrift."[272]

newly emerging peoples. An appropriate substitute for "non-whites," a term that is unacceptable because it implies that "white" is the standard all other skin colors should be measured against.

Nha. See: Ha.

nonaboriginal Australians. See: nonindigenous Americans.

noncanonical texts. Literary works, almost exclusively written by representatives of unempowered groups, that have been systematically marginalized or ignored by the white-male-dominated cadre of professors who control typical American university curricula.[273]

nondiscretionary fragrance. A natural body odor (as differentiated from an artificially applied one, such as perfume or cologne). To discriminate against persons whose nondiscretionary fragrance one deems "unpleasant"—as, for example, to refuse to sit next to them in a classroom, meeting, theater, airplane, or lunch counter—is to engage in **scentism.**[274] Example: *"I sense the* **nondiscretionary fragrance** *of a rodent-American,"* *observed the suspicious—and multiculturally alert—detective.* See: **discretionary fragrance.**

nonemerging peoples. National, ethnic, or creedal groups which have suffered total genocide, such as the Aztecs, the Tainos, and the Carthaginians.[275] Also: **no-longer emerging peoples.**

non-goal-oriented members of society. A nonjudgmental term for those who were once dismissed as "bums."[276]

nonhuman animal. A term popularized by the animal rights movement to remind humans that they, too, are a species of animal, no better or worse than any other.[277] Also: **nonhuman being.**

nonhuman-animal speciesism. Noting that animal rights philosopher Peter Singer has defined "speciesists" as those who "allow the interests of their own species to override the greater interests of members of other species," *U.S. News & World Report* columnist John Leo argues that nonhuman beings ought to be held to the same standard as human ones. "A snake eating a bird" would be a speciesist, writes Leo. "So would...a jackal eating a snake or a lion eating Peter Singer."[278]

nonindigenous Americans. Everyone living on U.S. soil except those descended from precolonial peoples. The term was instituted to emphasize the point that white European immigrants have no right to use terms such as "nonwhite" to marginalize populations whose presence in the Western Hemisphere predates their own by many centuries. Former Australian Prime Minister Bob Hawke employed a similar coinage in March 1992 when he talked about his dream of having "aboriginal Australians and **nonaboriginal Australians** holding hands by the millennium."[279]

nonliving person. A culturally sensitive synonym for "corpse" popularized by the *New England Journal of Medicine*.[280] Example: *The fact that Norman Mailer elected not to title his famous war novel* The Underclothed and the **Nonliving** *was an early clue to his gross insensitivity.*

nontraditional-age student. A nonageist term for an individual whose undergraduate education was interrupted and who returns to school at a later date to complete it.[281]

nontraditionally ordered. Sloppy; disorganized.[282]

nontraditional shopper. Looter, shoplifter.[283]

Nontraditional shoppers *spontaneously displaying their dissatisfaction with socioeconomic conditions in South Central Los Angeles, April 1992.*

nonvagrant homed. People who, for the moment at least, are not homeless. The term was coined to counteract the prevailing notion that those privileged enough to have a place to live are the "standard," while those who happen to have no permanent residence are somehow "deviant."[284] Also: **temporarily homed.**

nonviolent food. Food which is obtained without killing, injuring, or inconveniencing nonhuman animals.[285] Example: *"After a tiring but productive afternoon of tree-spiking,"* said Rudy [*not his real name!*], *"nothing beats a delicious* **nonviolent** *dinner!"*

nonwaged. Unemployed.[286] See also: **in an orderly transition between career changes; indefinitely idled; involuntarily leisured; occupationally dispossessed; vocationally deprived.**

O occupationally dispossessed. Unemployed.[287] See also: **in an orderly transition between career changes; indefinitely idled; involuntarily leisured; nonwaged; vocationally deprived.**

oppressed-within-the-oppressed status. The relative amount of oppression suffered by any of the various communities within an underrepresented identity group.[288] For example, both African-American men and African-American women are racism and classism survivors, but African-American women are victimized by sexism as well. Indeed, if hierarchical thinking were permissible, the late writer Audre Lorde, who defined herself as "a forty-nine-year-old Black lesbian feminist socialist mother of two, including one boy, and a member of an interracial couple,"[289] would have been a leading candidate for recognition as the single most oppressed human being in the United States. See: **oppression.**

oppression. The discrimination against or suppression of individuals or groups, on the basis of what the Smith College Office of Student Affairs calls "stereotypes, generalizations and attitudes (conscious or unconscious)." Unless one possesses **institutional power**, the Smith Office points out, the means to discriminate against entire groups of people are unavailable.[290] It follows, then, that in the United States, only whites—specifically, Eurocentric heterosexual white males—can, and do, behave oppressively.

optically inconvenienced. Nearsighted, for example, or farsighted, or blind. Example: *"I'm tired of Cattle Oppressors and Native Americans," said Buddy. "Let's play a game of* **Optically Inconvenienced** *Individual's Bluff."* Also: **optically challenged**.[291]

orally challenged. Having a speech impediment; mute. See also: vocally challenged.

orthographically challenged. An appropriately sensitive term for what used to be called "a poor speller."[292]

Former Vice President Dan Quayle,
an **orthographically challenged** *individual.*

orthopedically impaired. Having one or more damaged or missing limbs.[293]

*An **orthopedically impaired** bandit.*

other animals. A nonspeciesist term for fauna belonging to species other than one's own.[294] See also: **nonhuman animal.**

Otherness, otherness. The quality or qualities that make members of marginalized groups "different" from individuals in the mainstream of society.[295] The concept of "the Other" gained currency in the writings of the French existentialists, who saw it as a term of alienation. Today's multiculturalists, however, view the "celebration of otherness" as a vehicle for self-empowerment. See: **multiculturalism; politics of difference.**

outing. The tactic of exposing the hitherto secret membership of a public figure in the gay or lesbian community as an instrument of identity politics. (By contrast, the practice of revealing that a gay or lesbian separatist has covertly engaged in heterosexual relations is known as **inning.**)

ovarimony. Testimony. The term was coined, Francine Wattman Frank and Paula A. Treichler inform us, not only because of the etymological associations between the words "testimony" and "testes," but also as a protest against "the Islamic practice of regarding women's statements under oath as less valuable than men's."[296] Example: *"You are hereby ordered to appear in court to **ovarify** in the aforementioned case," read the language of the subvulva that the process server handed to Clarissa.*

ovarium. A term, popularized at the University of California at Santa Cruz, for any seminar where women are present.[297] See also: ovular.

overdetermined. A postmodernist term meaning, more or less, "insufficiently vague, and therefore boring."[298]

overexploited nations. Underdeveloped nations.[299]

ovular. A nonphallogeneric term for "seminar," recommended for use especially when women are amongst the attendees.[300] See also: ovarium. (Note: "Ovular" may also be used as a substitute for the word "seminal," which is to be avoided because it praises originality in relation to the male seed.[301])

Paradigm. A model, pattern, example, or "worldview" upon which a system is based or organized. The Earth First! movement's snappy slogan, "Subvert the dominant paradigm!" is therefore a call, not to reform the existing system, but, as movement cofounder Dave Foreman puts it, to seek totally "new (old) ways of organizing ourselves, turning away from hierarchy to tribalism."[302]

parasitically oppressed. Pregnant.[303]

parentheses. See: transgression strategy.

part white. The only correct label for describing individuals once commonly referred to as "part black," "part Native American," "part Asian," etc. These obsolete phrases are inappropriate because they assume that white is the standard.[304]

pathetic aesthetic. A form of art, described in the catalog for the 1993 Biennial Exhibition at New York City's Whitney Museum as "one of the most powerful developments among artists [of the] emerging generation." Pathetic aesthetic deliberately rejects such outmoded concepts as originality and coherence of form in order to celebrate the inept, the degraded, and the dysfunctional. Its "embrace of failure," the catalog continues, transforms "deficiencies into something positive. . . . The art is infused with meaning that reflects the disaffection of the socially marginalized, subcultural groups within a predominately white, male, heterosexual society." One of the leading proponents of pathetic aesthetic is Sue Williams, who, according to critic Lisa Phillips, uses her "probing, scathing wit" to expose the "heinous abuse, misogyny, neglect, rape, incest, and violence that permeates many sexual relations and social encounters." As an example of Williams's "probing, scathing wit," Phillips offers one of the artist's most celebrated works:

a painting emblazoned with the text: "The art world can suck my proverbial dick."[305] See also: **successism.**

patriarchy. Male-dominated and -controlled society, or, as Boston College philosopher/theologist Mary Daly defines it in *Gyn/Ecology,* the colonization of the universe by men.[306]

pedal sizism. The oppression of those whose feet are larger than the norm.[307]

The yeti, a survivor of **pedal-sizist** *oppression.*

Penthouse Animal Companion. Term for the women who pose for *Penthouse* magazine, suggested by University of California professor Roderick Nash during an environmental ethics lecture. A group of Nash's students immediately filed an official sexual harassment charge against him.[308]

"people first" wordings. See: person of color.

people with differing abilities. B. Freer Freeman's winning entry in the "Create a New Word" contest, which was sponsored by the National Cristina Foundation with the aim of finding "a word or phrase which focuses on the *abilities* of people with disabilities."[309] Freeman's winning phrase earned him a prize of $50,000—an amount which some spoilsports in the disability rights movement, obviously unfamiliar with the **Sapir-Whorf Hypothesis,** suggested might better have been spent on concrete assistance for the people with differing abilities themselves. See: **severely euphemized.**

people with special needs. Individuals with a disability.

personhole. An ambigenic term for "manhole."[310] See also: **femhole; maintenance hatch; personnel access structure; utility hole.**

A **personhole.**

person living with AIDS. A recommended term—since it stresses the positive concept that AIDS is something that can be *lived* with—for an individual with acquired immune deficiency syndrome. Because of the widespread diseasism and homophobia connected with this condition, many prefer the two recognized abbreviations for this phrase—PLWA and PLA—to the term itself.[311]

personnel access structure. One of the many nonsexist improvements upon the word "manhole."[312] See also: **femhole; maintenance hatch; personhole; utility hole.**

*A **personnel access structure.***

person of color, person of Color. A non-white person.[313] This is an example of the "people first" wordings currently receiving praise in liberation politics circles. (Another, cited by Anne Matthews in the July 7, 1991, edition of *The New York Times,* is "woman with a disability" rather than "disabled woman."[314]) Before referring to someone as a "person of color," however, it's important to note that the Commission on the Status of Women Forum has declared the term unacceptable, on the grounds that it "obscures diversity and specificity and lumps all racial and ethnic groups together, thus facilitating the tendency in language to universalize."[315]

person of differing sobriety. A drunk.[316]

person of gender. A woman.[317]

person of noncolor. A white person, especially a white Anglo-Saxon Protestant.[318]

person of size. An obese person. Also: **larger-than-average citizen; person of substance.**

*Antoine Domino,
a **person of size** and color.*

person of substance. An "overweight" person.[319] Also: **larger-than-average citizen; person of size.**

personslaughter. Gender-fair improvement upon "manslaughter" suggested by language reformer Bobbye D. Sorrels. Sorrels, author of *The Nonsexist Communicator: Solving the Problems of Gender and Awkwardness in the English Language,* notes that "humanslaughter," "wo/manslaughter," and "manslaughter and womanslaughter" are also appropriate substitutes.[320]

persons presenting themselves as commodity allotments within a business doctrine. A nonjudgmental substitute for "prostitutes," used in a proposal for a rehabilitative "safe house" submitted by the city of Allentown, Pennsylvania.[321] Example: *"Hey, handsome—if you'll pardon the lookist lingo,"* said the scantily clad yet culturally sensitive person who was presenting herself as a commodity allotment within a business doctrine, *"if you're looking for a good time, I'm the sex care provider for you!"* See also: sex care provider; sexual surrogacy; sex worker.

persons with difficult-to-meet needs. Serial killers, for example.

Charles Manson, a **person with difficult-to-meet needs.**

phallocentrism. The belief that male generative power is, and should be, the driving force of society[322]; the tendency of white males to view all other groups and cultures from the point of view of their sexual organs. Example: *It was* **phallocentric**—*not to mention sexist, lookist, and speciesist—of Rod to exclaim, "Man, that girl is a dog!"*

phallocracy. A form of government or society, in which—to use B Ruby Rich's memorable phrase—"men follow the arc of transcendence emanating from their cocks to build culture and civilization."[323]

phallogeneric term. "A pseudogeneric term which, while pretending to include women, in reality conveys the message that only men exist" (as defined by Mary Daly in *Websters' First New Intergalactic Wickedary of the English Language*).[324] Examples: *man; mankind;* and the pronoun *he*, when used generically.

phallogocentrism. The use, by white, heterosexual males, of such discredited devices as reasoning and logic to maintain a position of sexual and political dominance.[325]

pharmacological preference. Drug addiction.[326]

photo-insensitive. A term coined to describe those who insist on using flash cameras in public despite the evidence that flashing lights can be a potential trigger for epileptic seizures.[327] In response to the growing national outcry against photo-insensitivity, the first National Lesbian Conference in Atlanta, Georgia, banned flash cameras from its proceedings.[328]

phylumism. The belief that one's particular class of organism is inherently superior to another because of the supposed greater sophistication of its body plan.[329] Example: *Jennifer held the* **phylumistic** *conviction that she was better than a steamer clam just because she had a well-developed endoskeleton instead of a bivalve shell.*

The steamer clam, a defenseless victim of **phylumism.**

physically challenged. A cruelty-free synonym for "physically disabled."[330]

physically different. A more sensitive substitute for "physically disabled."[331]

PLA and **PLWA.** The two recognized abbreviations for "person living with AIDS," considered by many to be the preferred term for referring to an individual with acquired immune deficiency syndrome.[332] See: **person living with AIDS**.

pluralism. The movement to reshape society so that heretofore oppressed groups can participate fully without sacrificing their cultural identities.[333] See: **multiculturalism**.

Pn. Abbreviation for "Person"—a nonsexist, gender-free substitute for the titles "Ms." and "Mr.," advocated by Varda One, publisher of the Los Angeles–based newspaper *Everywoman*.[334] Example: *Todd's favorite politically correct canonical novel was* Goodbye, Pn. Chips.

politics of difference. The growing movement among groups outside the mainstream to use their collective identity as a vehicle for self-empowerment; to celebrate, rather than apologize for, their "otherness"; to assert what makes them "different," rather than attempting to assimilate themselves, or permit themselves to be assimilated, into a homogenized mass culture. Also called **identity politics**.

pomo. A popular slang term meaning "postmodern," "an adherent of postmodernism," or "postmodernism" itself, coined as a self-referential illustration of what good fun the postmodernist movement can be.[335] See: **postmodernism**.

postmodernism. A movement whose view of society provides a theoretical basis for much of what has come to be known as "politically correct" thought. According to Pauline Marie Rosenau, author of *Post-Modernism and the Social Sciences,* **pomo** (as it's affectionately called by its adherents) "questions the validity of modern science and the notion of objective knowledge,…discards history, rejects humanism, and resists any truth claims." In political science, it "calls into question the authority of hierarchical, bureaucratic decision-making structures." In anthropology "it inspires the protection of local, primitive cultures from First

World attempts to reorganize them." In addition, Rosenau points out, postmodernism has spawned a whole "new generation of social movements, ranging from New Age sensitivities to Third World fundamentalism."[336]

preliterate. An arguably nonjudgmental term for describing a culture that has not developed written language. "Preliterate" is more politically correct than "nonliterate," according to William Safire, because it assumes that literacy is "right around the corner." However, as Amoja Three Rivers points out in *Cultural Etiquette: A Guide for the Well-Intentioned,* the assumption that cultures based on the oral rather than the written tradition are backward is a modern Eurocentric prejudice. Therefore, use of the term "preliterate," which reflects this prejudice, has become a matter of considerable controversy.[337]

previously enjoyed sound bite. A cliché.[338]

prewoman. Young girl (as defined by cartoonist Jeff Sheshol).[339]

Prewomen.

privileges. Defined by Lewis Lapham, in *Harper's Magazine,* as "monocultural advantages belonging to people whom one doesn't like."[340] See: **rights.**

privileging. Giving special attention, or priority, to an opinion, a person, a theory, an argument, a group, a perspective, a paradigm, or a text. Privileging is a cardinal sin both of multicultural politics and postmodernist criticism.[341]

processed animal carcasses. Meat, labeled honestly at last so that the insensitive human animals who insist on eating it must come to terms with their cruelty. Other acceptable terms for meat include **scorched animal corpses** and just plain flesh.[342]

processed tree carcasses. Books, newspapers, paper bags, and any other byproducts of the dominant culture's pillage of the Earth's forests.[343]

Tom Brown at Oxford, *a* **processed tree carcass.**

pro-choice. In favor of the legal right to an abortion.

protector. Nonspeciesist alternative to **companion animal**.[344]

A human animal being attacked by her **protector.**

PWA. Abbreviation for "person with AIDS." While "PWA" is considered an unexceptionable way of referring to individuals with acquired immune deficiency syndrome, **PLWA** and **PLA**, abbreviations for "person living with AIDS," are more "optimistic" terms, and are thus preferred by many.[345]

Q **queer.** See: gay.

Racism. "The belief that one group of people are superior to another and therefore have the right to dominate, and power to institute and enforce their prejudices and discriminations" (as defined by the Smith College Office of Student Affairs).[346]

racist! A politically correct way of saying "I disagree with you on that!" (as defined by *U.S. News & World Report* columnist John Leo).[347]

realmism. See: kingdomism.

receptive noninitiator. A man guilty of reciprocating the sexual advances of, or allowing himself to be seduced by, a woman in a subordinate position to himself. According to Sue Rosenberg Zalk, the Director of the Center for the Study of Women and Society at the State University of New York, the unequal power relationship means that the receptive noninitiator's "concession" to the woman's overtures is a clear example of sexual harassment. "So what?" she quotes the hypothetical receptive noninitiator as saying to himself. "She was the seducer. I put no pressure on her." This, Zalk tells us, is "a transparent rationalization." The fact that the woman "asked," she points out, "is not an explanation for why he complied." "A woman would never get away with offering such an excuse," she concludes.[348]

reclaim. To take back something—one's power, one's pride, one's literature, one's bioregion, one's mythology, one's language—that has been stolen, perverted, or suppressed by the dominant culture. (Note: It is perfectly possible for a group to reclaim something it never possessed to begin with, since it undoubtedly would have had it, were it not for the dehumanizing effects of systematic oppression.)[349]

rectocentrism. The belief that right-handed people, being the majority, have the right to dictate the design of the human environment for their sole convenience, disregarding the needs of left-handed people.[350] Example: *Not one big-league pitcher is named "Righty" or referred to as a "northpaw"—two unfortunate manifestations of the* **rectocentrism** *infecting professional sports.* See: sinistromanualism.

rights. Defined by Lewis Lapham, in *Harper's Magazine,* as "monocultural advantages belonging to oneself or one's friends."[351] See: **privileges**.

"right-to-be-sheltered" laws. A term characterizing ordinances such as the New York City ruling that the local government has no authority to deny a free bed to anyone who requests one.[352]

"right-to-not-be-sheltered" laws. A term characterizing ordinances such as the New York City ruling that the local government has no authority to insist that anyone give up sleeping in the street in exchange for a free bed.[353]

Sapir-Whorf Hypothesis. The theory, proposed by Edward Sapir and Benjamin Lee Whorf, that all human culture is fabricated by language, and that therefore, before we can change a pattern of behavior, we must change the terms which relate to it.[354] It was the Sapir-Whorf Hypothesis, of course, which made the publication of this dictionary a near-sacred mission for the American Hyphen Society.

scentism. Imposing one's **discretionary fragrance**—perfume, cologne, shaving cream, etc.—on those who do not wish to smell it. Antiscentist activists have proposed the setting up of **fragrance-free zones** in public gathering places, with sniffers (*U.S. News & World Report* columnist John Leo calls them "**aroma police**"[355]) stationed at the perimeter to prevent violations. Not to be confused with **smellism**.

scorched corpses of animals. How *Washington Post* columnist Colman McCarthy, using terminology originally proposed by George Bernard Shaw, suggests supermarkets might be required by truth-in-labeling laws to advertise "gourmet-trim beef rib steak, Smok-a-Rama sliced bacon or oven-stuffer whole roasters."[356] See: **flesh; processed animal carcasses**.

seamstron. A nongender-marked synonym for "seamstress."[357] See: sewer; waitron.

Betsy Ross, a **seamstron.**

seasonal employee. Migrant worker.[358]

seasoned. Old. See also: longer-living; mature; senior; chronologically gifted; experientially enhanced.[359]

second baseperson. See first baseperson.

seductron. Seducer or seductress.[360] Example: *"Only when receptive noninitiators stop oppressing* **seductrons,**" *announced Paula,* "*can society be said to be truly sexually free.*" See: **waitron.**

Circe, a **seductron***, in the company of two temporarily nonhuman animal companions.*

sefem. One of the very few coinages made possible by replacing "man" or "men" with "fem" that was not included by Bina Goldfield in her ovular work, *The Efemcipated English Handbook.* Arriving at a broadly accepted definition for the term is one of the great unmet challenges of the language reform movement. See: **wofem.**

self-naming. See: Asian-American.

senior. Old.[361] See also: **longer-living; mature; seasoned; chronologically gifted; experientially enhanced.**

separatism. A personal and political movement whose proponents seek self-empowerment by refusing to associate with males, heterosexual females, or lesbians with male children. "It is always the pleasure of the master to enter the slave's hut," Marilyn Frye has written. "The slave who decides to exclude the master from her hut is declaring herself not a slave."[362]

severely euphemized. Disabled. The term Andrew J. Washburn, in the Winter 1990 issue of *The Disability Rag* magazine, elected "the best response so far" to a contest, announced by the National Cristina Foundation, to coin new, positive phrases, along the lines of **differently abled** and **handi-capable**, for people with disabilities.[363] See: **people with differing abilities.**

sewer. A term recommended by Val Dumond, author of *The Elements of Nonsexist Usage,* as a gender-free improvement upon "seamstress."[364] See also: **seamstron.**

sex care provider. A prostitute, as characterized on a 1991 PBS broadcast on the subject of AIDS.[365] See also: **sex worker; sexual surrogacy; persons presenting themselves as commodity allotments within a business doctrine.**

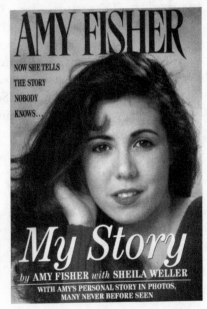

AMY FISHER

NOW SHE TELLS THE STORY NOBODY KNOWS...

My Story

by AMY FISHER *with* SHEILA WELLER

WITH AMY'S PERSONAL STORY IN PHOTOS, MANY NEVER BEFORE SEEN

*A processed tree carcass by Amy Fisher, a former **sex care provider**, who in 1992 became a guest of the correctional system.*

sexism. "Stereotyping of males and females on the basis of their gender; the oppression of women by society in the belief that gender is an indication of ability" (as defined by the Smith College Office of Student Affairs).[366] Example: *"Ol' Man River," the so-called "Negro work song" Jerome Kern and Oscar Hammerstein II wrote for* Show Boat, *is racist, ageist, and* **sexist***."*

sexually active. Nonjudgmental term for "promiscuous."[367]

sexually dysfunctional. Perverted.[368]

sexual surrogacy. A Fort Lauderdale defense attorney's term for "prostitution."[369] See also: **sex care provider; sex worker; persons presenting themselves as commodity allotments within a business doctrine.**

sexual terrorism. Defined by John Stollenberg, author of *Refusing to Be a Man,* as one of the two means by which the male sex "flourishes" as a political entity. The other is "acts of force."[370]

sex worker. The preferred occupational title for "prostitute."[371] The term "prostitute" is inappropriate, not only because it is judgmental, but because, as Dr. Dale Spender points out in *Women of Ideas and What Men Have Done to Them,* it is extremely difficult to define it without including "wives," who "also exchange sexual services in return for support."[372] See also: **sex care provider; sexual surrogacy; persons presenting themselves as commodity allotments within a business doctrine.**

she-ro. A term coined by Maya Angelou to replace "hero," which, through longtime usage, has come to embody masculine values.[373] See also: **hera.**

significant other. Husband; lover; spouse; wife; girlfriend; boyfriend; sex partner.[374]

sinistromanualism. The discrimination against, or oppression of, the left-handed minority by the right-handed majority. [375] See: **rectocentrism.**

sinistromanualistic language. Language that stigmatizes, is offensive to, or discriminates against people who are left-handed. As the noted left-handed activist James Lipton has pointed out, English is full of sinistromanualistic words and phrases: "left-handed compliment," "having two left hands," "left out," "gauche," and "sinister," just to name a few. Similarly, "rectitude," "righteous," "right-minded," "upright," "dextrous," "adroit," and even "right" itself are words that unfairly privilege the right-handed majority.[376] All such words and phrases should be carefully avoided.

size-friendly. Furniture or clothing, for example, into which a **person of substance** can fit comfortably. [377] See also: **generously cut.**

*A larger-than-average citizen being fitted for a **size-friendly** garment.*

sizeism. Discrimination by the temporarily fit against those who, to quote *A Feminist Dictionary*, "weigh more than the fashion, entertainment, and health industries say is appropriate."[378] Also: **fatism; weightism.**

skin-color genetically dominant. Of color.[379] See: **skin-color genetically dominant world majority.**

skin-color genetically dominant world majority. A term for "people of color," coined to celebrate the fact that the skin-melanization gene is dominant. As Jawanza Kunjufu points out in *Countering the Conspiracy to Destroy Black Boys*, "When you consider an African man, African woman, European man and European woman, there are four possible heterosexual combinations, but only one [European man–European woman] will produce a child with a similar genetic makeup to Europeans."[380] It is culturally appropriate to refer to people of color as **members of the skin-color genetically dominant world majority.** See also: **mutant albino genetic-recessive global minority.**

skin-melaninated.   A synonym for "of color" frequently encountered in the writings of psychiatrist Frances Cress Welsing, author of *The Cress Theory of Color Confrontation and Racism.*[381]

smellism.   Discrimination against, or stigmatization or oppression of, a human or nonhuman being because his/her/its nondiscretionary body odor is deemed to be unpleasant—for example, electing not to sit next to her, him, or it on a crowded bus. Example: *It was very* **smellist** *of Joe to yell, "The Yankees stink!"* Not to be confused with **scentism.**

snow person.   A gender-fair replacement for snowman, recommended by Val Dumond in *The Elements of Nonsexist Usage.* Dumond also favors the term snow creation.[382]

sobriety-deprived.   Intoxicated. See also: **chemically inconvenienced.**[383]

socially misaligned.   Psychotic.[384] Example: *Jeffrey Dahmer, who just happens to be* **socially misaligned,** *was detained in Milwaukee in connection with the nonviability of from ten to seventeen African-Americans of undetermined sexual preference.*

sorceron.   Ambigenic term for sorcerer/sorceress.[385]

Morgan le Fay, a **sorceron.**

special. Physically or mentally disabled. As is the case with **exceptional**, the term is still widely used, but is gradually being supplanted by **physically challenged, mentally challenged,** and **differently abled,** which many consider to be more positively cast.[386]

specially organized. Sloppy.[387]

specially skilled. See: **uniquely proficient.**

speciesism. Oppression (e.g., slaughtering, eating, etc.) of nonhuman animals by the dominant species in the belief that the dominant way of doing things is the superior way. As an antidote to speciesism, veal was removed from the menu of the Vassar Student Union.[388]

speciesistic dualism. The insistence that the differences between human and nonhuman animals are more important than the similarities, and that, therefore, nonhumans must be confined to a category utterly distinct from our own. As Dr. Neal D. Barnard, president of the Physician's Committee for Responsible Medicine, points out, this sort of "good vs. bad, us vs. them" thinking "leads to the use of preferences (e.g. rat vs. baby) rather than morally relevant criteria as a basis for ethical decisions."[389]

The spider, a voiceless victim of **speciesistic dualism**.

spinster's degree. A new name for the master's degree, coined by Cheris Kramarae and Mercilee M. Jenkins to alert readers to "the traditional attention accorded the male side of the gender-linked terms."[390]

spiritually dysfunctional. An appropriately sensitive term for "suicidal," used by *The San Diego Union-Tribune* to describe a woman who terminally inconvenienced herself during the summer of 1992.[391] See also: **autoeuthanasia, voluntary death.**

spontaneous display of community dissatisfaction with prevailing socioeconomic conditions. An appropriately sensitive term for "riot."[392]

spouse equivalent. Any significant other to whom one is not married.[393] See also: **domestic partner.**

stolen products. Products, such as eggs, milk, cheese, honey, and wool, taken from nonhuman animals by human ones. The use of such items, even when they are obtained in a "humane" manner,

Stolen products.

is increasingly regarded as an unconscionable violation of nonhuman animal rights.[394] Example: *The politically correct nutritionist outlined the four basic food groups: 1.* **Stolen products.** *2. Brutally betrayed botanical companions. 3. Hapless victims of speciesist slaughter. 4. Fortuitarian comestibles.* Also: **stolen nonhuman-animal products.**

straw person. Gender-inclusive improvement upon "straw man."[395]

street harassment. Girl watching.[396]

street orientation. Housebreaking.[397] Example: *Suki joined her dog friend for a mutually nurturing* **street orientation** *session.* (Note: While enjoying increasing favor among animal rights advocates, the concept of street orientation has run afoul of the environmental movement.)

substance abusers. Drug addicts and drunks, for example.[398]

substandard housing. Slum.[399]

successism. The dominant culture tendency to value certain members of society more highly than others simply because, through the diligent application of their knowledge, talents, and abilities, they happen to have achieved respect, recognition, position, and/or economic security.[400] As a reaction against the successism rampant in white male heterosexual society, a powerful new art form known as **pathetic aesthetic** has emerged, which, according to the Whitney Museum's 1993 Biennial Exhibition catalog, uses such techniques as unoriginality and apparent ineptitude to reflect "the feeling of inadequacy engendered by repressive social structures."[401]

sun people. Africans, Asians, and natives of Latin America and the Caribbean. The term was coined by Dr. Leonard Jeffries, chairman [sic] of the Afro-American Studies Department of the City University of New York, who theorizes that humanity is divided into two principal groups, "sun people" and "ice people" (the European-American descendants of northern Ice Age peoples). The two groups have diametrically opposed value systems: ice people are materialistic, egotistical, and exploitative, while sun people are humanistic, communal, and caring.[402] See also: **snow person.**

Idi Amin,
a sun person.

survivor. Victim. Survivor is the more appropriate term because it emphasizes the active courage, rather than the passive subjugation, of the person in question.[403] Example: *Typhoid Mary, who just happened to infect thousands of people, was herself a diseasism* **survivor.**

symbolic annihilation of women. Too much media coverage of men, for example. [404]

T **TAB.** A temporarily able-bodied person.[405] See: **temporarily able.**

technologically challenged. Computer illiterate.[406]

tem. See: **tey.**

temporally challenged. Chronically late.[407]

temporarily able. Having no physical or mental disabilities.[408] Also: **temporarily able-bodied** (often used in its acronymic form, TAB). These terms are important, Sonia Osman tells us in *Spare Rib* magazine, "because disabilities are an issue for all, not just because many will (for instance) lose our hearing and our mobility if we live long enough, but because notions of having to have 'perfect' bodies disable us all."[409]

temporarily homed. See: **nonvagrant homed.**

temporarily metabolically abled. Alive.[410]

temporarily misoriented. Lost.[411]

temptron. Temptress or tempter.[412] See: **waitron.**

Salome, a **temptron.** *Also pictured (counterclockwise from top) are her stepfather, King Herod; a companion animal; and the no-longer-viable head of John the Baptist.*

ter. See: **tey.**

terminally inconvenienced. Dead.[413] Example: *"If you're not out of town by noon, bull/cow oppressor,"* said the Sheriff, *"you're a* **terminally inconvenienced** *individual."*

testosterone poisoning. The hormonal imbalance suffered by so-called "normal" males.[414]

text. The only correct term for a book, poem, ad, poster, television program, or anything else that appears to convey information. A proper comprehension of postmodernism is impossible until one realizes that *all* events, *all* phenomena, are texts.[415]

text tallying. The monitoring of an individual's writings and utterances to determine her/his adherence, or nonadherence, to a professed political orthodoxy. For example, B Ruby Rich wrote, in a *Village Voice* profile of Camille Paglia, author of *Sexual Personae:* "Paglia should be put on notice that her texts are being tallied, and the hypocrisy is showing."[416]

tey, ter, *and* **tem.** The so-called "human" pronouns—first offered in 1972 as gender-free improvements upon "she," "he"; "her," "his"; and "her," "him," respectively.[417] Example: **Tey** *told* **tem** *that after* **tey** *tied* **ter** *tie,* **tey** *would tie* **ter** *tie for* **tem,** *too.* See also: **coself.**

third baseperson. See **first baseperson.**

totally challenged. Karen Ann Quinlan, for example.[418]

transgression strategy. A lit-crit term for any of various means of challenging conventional, dominant culture assumptions. A typical transgression strategy is breaking up a word with parentheses to highlight its different meanings and parts, or, as H. Aram Veeser of Wichita State University prefers to put it, to make it "deconstruct itself on the page."[419] Example: *Writing "deconstruction" as "de(con)struction" demonstrates the use of a* **transgression strategy.**

tree-spiking. See: **ecotage.**

Turtle Island. A name given by indigenous peoples to the continent now known as North America. The term is once again coming into favor, especially among bioregionalists and other deep ecologists.[420]

two-party sexual system. Western culture's nature-defying commitment to the idea that there are only two sexes. As Brown University geneticist, medical science professor, and intersexual rights advocate Anne Fausto-Sterling points out, "there are many gradations running from female to male; along that spectrum lie at least five sexes—perhaps even more."[421] See also: **ferms, herms,** and **merms.**

U

underhoused. Homeless. The term was coined by City Councilman John Oliver of Foster City, California, who, having no permanent domicile, sleeps in his camper truck.[422] See also: **houseless; involuntarily undomiciled.**

underrepresented groups. Everybody except white heterosexual males.[423]

uniquely abled. Disabled.[424]

uniquely coordinated. Clumsy.[425]

uniquely proficient. Incompetent.[426] Also: **differently qualified; specially skilled.**

unpaid sex worker. Wife or girlfriend.[427] Example: *"You won't get warts if you kiss a nonhuman amphibian animal,"* protested Kira. *"That's just a longer-lived* **unpaid sex worker**'s *tale."* See: **sex worker.**

unpremisesed businessperson. Sidewalk peddler (a crack dealer, for example).[428]

unwaged labor. Domestic chores, housework, child rearing, and (no pun intended) child bearing.[429]

utensil sanitizer. Dish washer.[430]

utility hole. A nongender-biased alternative to "manhole."[431] See also: femhole; maintenance hatch; personhole; personnel access structure.

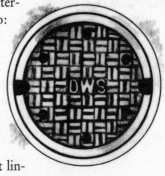

A **utility hole.**

V

vagina gratitude. Feminist linguist Dale Spender offers this as "a good corrective in a society which has only, and falsely, named 'penis envy.'" "[T]he renaming of sexuality in woman-centered, and not necessarily heterosexual, terms," she adds, "...will certainly make it difficult, if not impossible, for men to retain an image of their own supremacist sexuality...."[432] Example: *Whenever Sherrye saw a picture of a dramatic vulvic symbol like the Colosseum or the Mt. Blanc tunnel, she was filled with an overwhelming sense of* **vagina gratitude**. See also: **womb envy.**

ve, vis, *and* **ver.** Nongender-differentiated pronouns offered by Varda One, the editor of *Everywoman* magazine, to replace "she/he," "her/his," and "her/him," respectively.[433] Example: **Ve** *advised* **ver vis** *wish was* **vis** *command.*

vegan. A person who, based on the conviction that human animals have no right to exert dominion over nonhuman ones, shuns all animal products. Vegans decline to eat not only animal flesh (meat, fish, fowl, etc.), but also products "stolen" from animals (e.g. eggs, milk, cheese, and honey), and they wear only nonleather shoes and nonwool clothing.[434] See: **lacto-ovo-vegetarianism.**

vehicle appearance specialist. Car washer.[435]

ver. See: **ve.**

vertically challenged. Shorter, or taller, than average.[436] Also: **vertically inconvenienced; vertically constrained.**[437]

Tom Thumb, a **vertically challenged** *person, entertains his friends, Queen Victoria and Prince Albert.*

vis. See: ve.

vocally challenged. Mute.[438] See also: **orally challenged.**

vocationally deprived. Unemployed.[439] See also: **in an orderly transition between career changes; indefinitely idled; involuntarily leisured; nonwaged; occupationally dispossessed.**

voiceless, the. Nonhuman animals, as defined by *The Animals' Voice* magazine, whose memorable, if ableist, motto is "Through me the dumb shall speak…"[440] Ecowarrior Dave Foreman strikes a similar chord when he asks, in the manner of the indigenous Oneida people: "Who speaks for Wolf? Orca? Gila Monster? Redcockaded Woodpecker? Bog Lemming? Big Bluestem? Oak? Mycorrhizal fungi? We must constantly extend the community to include all."[441]

voluntary death. A less judgmental substitute for "suicide."[442] See also: **autoeuthanasia; spiritually dysfunctional.**

Waitron. The *Random House Webster's College Dictionary* defines this trendsetting new term as "a person of either sex who waits on tables; waiter or waitress."[443] Example: "**Waitron**, *there's a nonhuman animal in my soup!*" Also: **waitperson; dining room attendant**.

weightism. Oppression of the obese by the trim, or the favoring of thin people over fat people, especially in the workplace.[444] See also: **fatism; sizeism**.

whitemale. An increasingly popular new compound denoting a genetically oppressive man or boy. "Whitemale" can be used as either a noun or an adjective.[445]

White Power Elite. The Establishment.[446]

whiteskin privilege. Defined by African-American lesbian feminist Audre Lorde as "a major prop" of the "patriarchal power system," which confronts white women with the "pitfall of being seduced into joining the oppressor under the pretense of sharing power." It is easy, explains Lorde, "for white women to believe the dangerous fantasy that if they are good enough, pretty enough, sweet enough, quiet enough, teach the children to behave, hate the right people, and marry the right men, then you will be allowed to co-exist with patriarchy in relative peace, at least until a man needs your job or the neighborhood rapist happens along." Lawrence Watson, Assistant Dean for Academic Administration at the Harvard Graduate School of Design, expands the definition of "whiteskin privilege" to include white people's unique ability to purchase Band-Aids that match their skin tone.[447]

white solipsism. Belief in, or practice of, the theory that only the white race is of any real importance. See: **colorblindness**.

wildlife preservation park, wildlife preservation center. Terms adopted by the New York Zoological Society in 1993 to describe its installations in the Bronx and Central Park, among others, on the grounds that the word "zoo" had taken on negative connotations through its usage in such sentences as "This city is a fucking zoo!"[448] Example: *This city is a fucking* **wildlife preservation center***!*

wimmin. Nonsexist substitute for "women," coined by the editors of the periodical *This Magazine is For, About, and By Young Wimmin,* who wrote in their first issue: "We have spelt it this way because we are not wo*men* and neither are we fe*male*.... You may find it trivial—it's just another part of the deep, very deep, rooted sexist attitudes."[449] The singular of "wimmin" is **womon.** Example: *After carefully considering a proposal to change the title of Louisa May Alcott's* Little Women *to* Vertically Constrained **Wimmin,** *the Committee for an Inclusive Curriculum finally decided to ban it altogether.* See also: **wimyn; wofem; womban; womon; womyn.**

wimyn. Alternate spelling of "womyn." Theresa Pellow-McCauley recommends that "wimyn" be used exclusively in the plural and that "womyn" be used only in the singular.[450] See also: **wimmin; wofem; womban; womon; womyn.**

wimyn-bonded wimyn. See: **women-identified women.**

wimyn-identified wimyn. See: **women-identified women.**

with. The *only* appropriate preposition for connecting a person with an ailment, disease, disability, or injury (e.g. , *an individual* **with** *arthritis, a person* **with** *a heart condition*). Such constructions as "suffering from" and "afflicted with" are offensive because they lead the temporarily able-bodied to see individuals with special needs or differing abilities as objects of pity rather than as human beings. Similarly, one should say a "person who **has** [a disability]" rather than a "person who is stricken with [a disability.]"[451]

wofem. Gender-fair substitute for "woman" proffered in 1983 by Bina Goldfield, author of *The Efemcipated English Handbook.*[452] While some of Goldfield's other coinages (e.g., "abdofem," "afemdfemt," "comfemcefemt," and "femagefemt") have been criticized as unwieldy, formulaic, and even "trivializing of the feminist movement," this one seems destined to retain its initial popularity. Example: *"I decline to ovarify,"* the **wofem** *declared, "on the basis of my Fifth Afemdfemt rights."* See also: **efemcipated; wimmin; wimyn; womban; womon; womyn.**

womage. To manage, especially when the managing is done by a woman.[453]

woman-identified. See: women-identified women.

womanism and **womanist.** Terms for "black feminism" and "black feminist" coined by novelist-essayist Alice Walker.[454]

wo/manslaughter. See: personslaughter.

womban. An alternate spelling for "woman," proposed by Una Stannard to dramatize the fact that men tend to see women only as baby-making machines.[455] See also: **wimmin; wimyn; wofem; womon; womyn.**

womb envy. Dr. Dale Spender's term for the male terror of being excluded from reproductive relations.[456] See also: **vagina gratitude.**

women-bonded women. See: women-identified women.

women-identified women. Lesbians. Also: **women-bonded women; wimyn-identified wimyn; gynocentric be-ings.**

womon. Woman, the singular of **wimmin.** Debbie Alicen, one of the early popularizers of this term, writes: "I deny the necessity and/or the desirability of [the connection of woman and man] and use the spellings womon/wimmin as one way of removing man from the picture."[457] See also: **wimmin; wimyn; wofem; womban; womyn.**

womyn. An alternate spelling of "women," used, the *Random House Webster's College Dictionary* tells us, "to avoid the suggestion of sexism in the sequence "m-e-n." "Womyn" can also be used in the singular, as a replacement for "woman." Indeed, Theresa

Pellow-McCauley has recommended that "womyn" should be an *exclusively* singular term, and that its plural should be "wimyn."[458] See also: **wimmin; wimyn; wofem; womban; womon.**

Z Zeus-as-rapist. The archtype of the early patriarchal rape-of-the-Goddess myths which, to quote Mary Daly, "symbolized the vanquishing of woman-identified society."[459]

Zeus-as-rapist

PART TWO

POLITICALLY INCORRECT/
POLITICALLY CORRECT
DICTIONARY

From **abominable snowman**
to **zoo guide**

A

abominable snowman. See Bigfoot.

actor/actress. Actron. Example: *Jaye Davidson was nominated for Best Supporting* **Actron** *for ter role in* The Crying Game, *but the Oscron was won by Gene Hackperson.*

Jaye Davidson, an **actron.**

addiction. Pharmacological preference.

adulterer/adulteress. Adulteron.[1]

affliction. Condition.

after-shave lotion. Discretionary fragrance.

airhead. Cerebro-atmospheric individual.

alcoholic. Substance abuse survivor; person of differing sobriety.

alimony. Back salary; reparations. "Alimony" is unacceptable because it fails to state categorically that the person receiving financial support is morally entitled to receive it.[2]

alive. Temporarily metabolically abled. Example: *"He's* **temporarily metabolically abled***!" enthused Dr. Frankenstein.*

all the king's men. Bobbye D. Sorrels, in *The Nonsexist Communicator: Solving the Problems of Gender and Awkwardness in Modern English*, suggests the more inclusive (and euphonious) "all the monarch's personnel."[3]

animal. Nonhuman animal; nonhuman being; other animal.

animal trainer. Interspecies communicator.

Interspecies communicators *Siegfried and Roy.*

anti-social. Difficult to serve.

B **bald.** Differently hirsute; follicularly challenged; hair disadvantaged.

ballboy. Ballchild. See: **batboy.**

batboy. Batchild. See: **ballboy.**

A **batchild.**

Bigfoot (yeti). Nonhuman pedal-sizism survivor.

biology department. The Berkeley Rhetoric Department offers the following alternative: "Where animals are tortured and then murdered to fulfill the sadistic fantasies of white male scientist lackeys of the imperialistic drug companies."[4]

black. African-American; sun person; member of the African Diaspora. The term "black" is to be avoided, Robert B. Moore explains in "Racist Stereotyping in the English Language," because "the symbolism of white as positive and black as negative are pervasive in our culture." "The definition of *black*," he adds, "includes 'without any moral light or goodness, evil, wicked, indicating disgrace, sinful,' while that of *white* includes 'morally pure, spotless, innocent, free from evil intent.'"[5]

blind. Unseeing; nonsighted; optically challenged; visually inconvenienced.

body odor. Nondiscretionary fragrance.

book. Processed tree carcass. According to postmodern literary theory, all processed tree carcasses are "texts." See also: **newspaper.**

boring. Differently interesting; charm-free.

boutonniere. Botanical companion. See also: **corsage; houseplant.**

boyfriend. Significant other; partner; companion; (in cases when he is not married to his partner) spouse equivalent. Example: *Todd's friend Vernon's favorite movie was* **The Spouse Equivalent,** *starring Twiggy.*

brotherhood. Siblinghood.[6]

brotherhood of man. Siblinghood of persons.[7]

bum. Non-goal-oriented member of society.

C

cannibal. Humanitarian.

car washer. Vehicle appearance specialist.

chairman. Chair; chairperson.

chairwoman. Chair; chairperson.

child rearing. The unpaid work of social reproduction of the labor force.[8]

chores, domestic. Unwaged labor.

cigarette smoking. Assault with a deadly weapon (as defined by *Harper's Magazine* editor Lewis H. Lapham).[9]

cliché. Previously-enjoyed sound bite.

clumsy. Uniquely coordinated.

cologne. Discretionary fragrance.

computer illiterate. Technologically challenged.

corpse. Nonliving person.

corsage. Botanical companion. See also: **boutonniere; house-plant.**

crazy. Emotionally different.

Crazy Eddie, an
emotionally different *individual.*

crippled. Differently abled; physically challenged; handi-capable. The adjective of choice to describe a *severely* handi-capable individual is "involved." Example: "*Damn, there goes engine number three—I don't know if she'll make it back to base!*" rasped the desperate (and sexist) pilot of the **involved** *bomber.*

culturally deprived. Culturally dispossessed. "Culturally deprived" is unacceptable because it implies that Eurocentric culture is preferable to that of the marginalized group that is supposedly being deprived; "culturally dispossessed," on the other hand, unmasks the assimilationist character of mainstream American society.

D **dead.** Terminally inconvenienced; nonviable[10]; no longer a factor.[11] (The Rhetoric Department of the University of California at Berkeley prefers "metabolically different.")

William Casey, a **terminally inconvenienced** *American.*

deaf. Aurally challenged; aurally inconvenienced.

deaf-mute. Aurally-orally challenged.

dirty old man. Sexually focused chronologically gifted individual.[12]

disabled. Differently abled; physically challenged; physically different, physically inconvenienced; handi-capable; uniquely abled; special; exceptional; acceptional; involved; and (according to *The Disability Rag* magazine) severely euphemized.[13]

disease. Condition.

dishonest. Ethically disoriented; morally different.

dish washer. Utensil sanitizer.

A **utensil sanitizer.**

disorganized. Nontraditionally ordered.

disruptive child. Child with an attention deficit disorder.[14]

dogcatcher. Animal welfare officer.[15]

dog trainer. Interspecies communicator.

domestic chores. Unwaged labor.

doorman. Access controller[16];
doorperson.

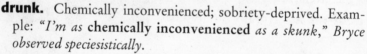

Access controllers.

drug addiction. Pharmacological
preference. Example: ATTENTION
ETHICALLY DISORIENTED INDIVIDU-
ALS AND PERSONS WITH A **PHAR-
MACOLOGICAL PREFERENCE:**
THERE IS NO RADIO IN THIS CAR
read the sign on the window of Heather's Volvo.

drunk. Chemically inconvenienced; sobriety-deprived. Example: *"I'm as* **chemically inconvenienced** *as a skunk," Bryce
observed speciesistically.*

Dutch treat, go. Pay one's own way. The term "Dutch treat,"
the University of Missouri's Journalism School's Multicultural
Management Fellows [sic] inform us, is unacceptable because it
"implies Dutch people are cheap."[17]

Economically disadvantaged. Economically exploited.

educational testing. Needs assessment.

egg. Stolen nonhuman-animal product. Example: *"Strips
of flesh cut from the slaughtered carcasses of cruelly exploited
nonhuman animals of the pig family and two* **nonhuman-**

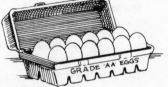

animal products stolen *from poultry, over easy!" shouted the waitron at the Biocentric Diner.*

Stolen nonhuman-animal products.

elderly. Mature; senior; chronologically gifted; longer-living; experientially enhanced.

emancipated. Efemcipated.

Eskimo, Alaskan. Native Alaskan; Alaskan native; indigenous Alaskan. More "politically correct" than any of these terms, however, are the names of the individual Native Alaskan groups: the principal ones are the Aleuts, the Yupiks, and the Inupats.

Eskimo, Canadian. Inuit.

Eskimo Pie™. Indigenous Alaskan Pie; Inuit popsicle.

Inuit popsicle.

Establishment, the. The white power elite.

evil. Morally different.

extra-large. Generously cut; having an easy, relaxed fit.[18]

F **fail (a course).** Achieve a deficiency.[19] Example: *"You have **achieved a deficiency** on your driving needs assessment," the Department of Motor Vehicles evaluator told Bryce as she extricated herself from the wreckage.*

failure (a person). Incompletely successful individual; individual with temporarily unmet objectives.

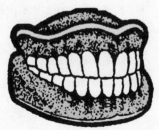

false teeth. Alternative dentation.

Alternative dentation.

farming. Exploiting mother earth.[20]

Exploiting mother earth.

farsighted.   Optically inconvenienced.

fat.   Big-boned[21]; horizontally challenged; differently sized; possessing an alternative body image. Example: *The Culturally Sensitive Circus featured such sights as The Most Vertically Inconvenienced Person in the World, The Fearless Interspecies Communicator and His Leonine Companion Animals, and the Womon with an* **Alternative Body Image**.

fatso.   Horizontally challenged person; person of size; person of substance; individual with an eating disorder[22]; sizeism survivor; weightism survivor; larger-than-average citizen.

fellowship.   Scholarship (when referring to a financial grant for academic study).[23]

fireman.   Firefighter; fireperson.

first baseman.   First baseperson.

fisherman.   The catchily named *Job Title Revisions to Eliminate Sex- and Age-Referent Language from the Dictionary of Occupational Titles,* published by the U.S. Department of Labor, recommends "fisher."[24] See also: **fishing**.

fishing.   Raping the planet's oceans, rivers, and/or lakes.[25] Example: *"Gone to* **rape the planet's oceans, rivers, and/or lakes**,*" read the hastily scribbled note Rod had left for his spouse equivalent.*

flunk out.   Have one's progress toward alternate life pursuits expedited (according to a 1991 memorandum issued by administrators at Wright State University in Dayton, Ohio).

freshmen. Frosh; first-year students; freshpersons; freshpeople.

frigid. Heterosexually celibate.

G

gender-blind. Gender-neutral.

gingerbread man. Gingerbread person[26]; gingerbread creation.

Gingerbread persons.

girl (twelve or older).
Woman. Nonsexist-language authorities Midge Lennert and Norma Willson note that "girl" is an unacceptable term for any female person aged twelve or older, or who has reached puberty.[27]

girl (eleven or younger). Prewoman.

girlfriend. Significant other; partner; companion; acquaintance rape survivor; unpaid sex worker; spouse equivalent (in cases when she is not married to her partner). For a discussion of the use of phrases such as "my significant other" or "my partner," see wife.

girl watching. Street harassment.

goof-off. Underachiever.[28]

graffiti. People's art.

grammar. Language reformer Betsy Warland defines it as "ethnocentric white patriarchal restructuring of language."[29]

gyp. Cheat. "Gyp" is unacceptable, according to the Multicultural Management Program Fellows [sic] of the University of Missouri Journalism School, because it is highly offensive to Gypsies, from whose name the word was derived.[30]

H **handicapped.** See: disabled.

he. Co; tey; ve.

heir/heiress. Inheritron.[31]

he-man. Tey-pn.[32]

henchman. Henchperson.[33] The American Hyphen Society also recommends **person of hench**.

her. (Objective) co; tem; ver. (Possessive) cos; ter; vis.

heroine. Hera; she-ro.

herpes. Hispes. Also: his 'n' herpes.

herself. Coself; temself; verself.

him. Co; tem; ver.

himself. Coself; temself; verself.

his. Cos; ter; vis.

Hispanic. Latino/Latina.

history. Herstory or hystery (especially when emphasizing the particular experience of women); his 'n' herstory (a gender-inclusive term suggested by columnist Peter Leo).

home economics. *A Woman's Thesaurus*, edited by Mary Ellen S. Capek, recommends "domestic arts." The University of Texas prefers "human ecology"—so much so that it changed the name of its "Department of Home Economics" to "Department of Human Ecology."[34]

homeless. Underhoused; involuntarily undomiciled. A Long Island teacher, quoted in *U.S. News & World Report*, prefers "houseless." "You are houseless but not homeless," she informed a group of local street people, "because home is wherever you are."

homosexual. Lesbian (women only); gay (men only).

honey. Stolen nonhuman-animal sweetener.

horsemanship. Temporarily possessed skill in the thievery of uncompensated nonhuman-animal transport.[35]

houseplant. Botanical companion. See also: **boutonniere; corsage.**

housewife. Domestic incarceration survivor; unwaged laborer; domestic artist; human ecologist.

A **domestic artist.**

housework. Unwaged labor.

human. Human animal; hufem; humyn.

humanity. "Animality" is the preferred nonspeciesist term.

hurricane. Himmicane.

husband. Significant other; partner; legalized rapist.

ignoramus. Knowledge-base nonpossessor.

illegal alien. To describe those who have recently entered the U.S.A. without "proper papers," the terms "undocumented worker" and "undocumented resident" are both considered appropriate.[36] Amoja Three Rivers notes, however, in *Cultural Etiquette: A Guide for the Well-Intentioned,* that the phrase "illegal alien" *is* acceptable in certain circumstances—for example, when referring to the Europeans and their descendants who illegally seized the continent in the first place.[37]

illiterate. Alternatively schooled.

impaired. Challenged; inconvenienced.[38]

Indian. Indigenous person; Native American. (Note: "Native American" has now fallen into some disrepute, according to *U.S. News & World Report* columnist John Leo, because it contains the word "American," which was derived from the "dread name" of a Eurocentric explorer, Amerigo Vespucci.)[39]

Indiana. Native Americana; Indigenous Persona.

Indian giver. European treaty-rights granter.[40]

Indian pudding. Indigenous pudding.[41]

insanity. Mental activity at the margin.

is. Just happens to be (when noting, for example, that a person is a member of an oppressed group).

J **janitor.** Environmental hygienist.

An **environmental hygienist.**

Jew. Jewish person. "Some people," say the Fellows [sic] of the University of Missouri Journalism School's Multicultural Management Program, "find the use of Jew alone offensive," and, therefore, it is to be avoided.[42]

jungle. Tropical rainforest. The word "jungle" is ideologically unsuitable because of its use in such insensitive phrases as "It's a goddamn jungle out there!" and because of its historical association with negative Eurocentric stereotypes of the African continent and its people.[43] Example: *"Kinesthetic movement period is over, children,"* called the teacher. *"Everybody off the* **tropical rainforest** *gym!"*

junkie. Person with a pharmacological preference; substance abuse survivor.

Kkingdom. Since kingdoms are never renamed "queendoms" when a woman accedes to the throne, many feminist linguists suggest this triumphally patriarchal term be shunned in favor of nonsex-linked words such as "realm" and "monarch." Example: *"A companion animal capable of providing personal transport, a companion animal capable of providing personal transport, my* **monarchy** *for a companion animal capable of providing personal transport!"*

know-nothing. See: ignoramus.

Llate (chronically). Temporally challenged.

lazy. Motivationally deficient; motivationally dispossessed.

lazybones. Person of torpor.[44]

long-winded. Alternatively concise.

looting. Nontraditional shopping.

loser. Uniquely-fortuned individual on an alternative career path; person with temporarily unmet objectives.

lost. Temporarily misoriented.

lover. Significant other; spouse equivalent; partner; acquaintance rape survivor. Example: *Although Brad was too shy to ask Dorothy to accompany him to* **Significant Others'** *Lane, he was nonetheless guilty of conceptual date rape.*

lumberjack. Tree butcher.[45]

Paul Bunyan, a mythical **tree butcher***, and his companion animal of color, Babe.*

M **Mafioso.** Member of a career-offender cartel.

maiden name. Birth family name.

mainstream. Dominant culture; malestream.[46]

malady. Condition.

manage. Womage (especially when the managing is being done by a woman).

manhole. Femhole; personhole; maintenance hatch; personnel access structure; utility hole.

man-made. Artificial; synthetic.[47]

manpower. Human resources.

manslaughter. Bobbye D. Sorrels, author of the appropriately subtitled *The Nonsexist Communicator: Solving the Problems of Gender and Awkwardness in the English Language*, suggests that "manslaughter" should be replaced by the more gender-fair "humanslaughter," "personslaughter," "wo/manslaughter," or "manslaughter and womanslaughter."

marriage. Domestic incarceration; legalized rape[48]; legalized prostitution.[49]

master (of what was formerly called a "pet"). According to the American Humane Society, the correct term is "human companion of a nonhuman companion."

masterful. Msterful.

master's degree. Spinster's degree.

masturbation (female). Msturbation.

meat. Flesh; processed animal carcasses; scorched corpses of animals—accurate terms that, unlike the euphemistic "meat," are

A waitron serving the **scorched corpses of a nonhuman being.**

designed to force flesh-eaters to face their cruelty to nonhuman beings.

meat-eater. Flesh-eater.[50]

menstruate. Femstruate.

mentally retarded. Special; exceptional; acceptional; mentally challenged; developmentally challenged; developmentally inconvenienced; developmentally different.

migrant worker. Seasonal employee.

milk. Stolen nonhuman-animal product.

milkman. Milkperson; stolen nonhuman-animal product deliverer.

A **stolen nonhuman-animal product deliverer.**

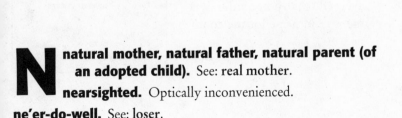

minority groups. Members of the world's majorities[51]; emergent groups; traditionally underrepresented communities.

misbehave. Engage in negative attention getting.[52]

mistress. Mstress, mstron, pntron.

motherfucker. Fatherencloser; fatherengulfer.[53]

mute. Vocally challenged; orally challenged.

N **natural mother, natural father, natural parent (of an adopted child).** See: real mother.

nearsighted. Optically inconvenienced.

ne'er-do-well. See: loser.

newspaper. Processed tree carcass. See also: **book; paper bag**.

An unwaged nonhuman-animal laborer delivering a **processed tree carcass.**

nonsexist. An adequate, if negatively-cast, term. But feminist linguist and word-maker Suzanne Elgin has a more positive one to offer—"ambigenic"—and others prefer the word "epicene."

nonwhite. Of color; oppressed; emergent; diasporan; skin-melaninated; newly-emerging (when describing a race or ethnic group). Until recently, the term "third world" was also considered acceptable, but its inherent implication that "first worlders"—that is, white Americans and Europeans—are somehow superior has caused it to fall into disrepute.

nonwhite individual. Person of color; person of Color; emergent person; sun person; member of the skin-color genetically dominant world majority.

North America. Turtle Island. Since "Turtle Island" was a label bestowed on North America by indigenous peoples long before the first Europeans arrived, many consider it a more valid name for the continent.

Turtle Island.

O **old.** Mature; seasoned; senior; longer-living; chronologically gifted; experientially enhanced.

old age. Maturity. The Fellows [sic] of the University of Missouri School of Journalism's Multicultural Management Program warn us that the seemingly innocent term "golden years" is *not* an acceptable substitute for the phrase "old age," since it falsely implies that people's later years are "uniformly idyllic."[54]

old joke. An ageist phrase disparaging longevity. The term of choice is "previously recounted humorous narrative."[55]

Oriental. Asian-American (when describing U.S. citizens of Asian descent). "Oriental" is "derogatory," according to the Smith College Office of Student Affairs, because it was not a self-chosen name: in coining the term "Oriental" to describe Asians, Europeans were oppressing them by usurping the power to define who they were. Indeed, suggests columnist John Leo, "all college departments of 'Oriental studies' that do not wish to be burned down in the name of tolerance should rename themselves rather quickly."[56]

owner (of what was formerly called a "pet"). The American Humane Society says the appropriate term is "human companion of a nonhuman companion."

P **panhandler.** Unaffiliated applicant for private-sector funding.[57] See also: **panhandling**.

panhandling. Random solicitation of informal sources of interim financing for a personal economic recovery program.[58] See also: **panhandler**.

paper bag. Processed tree carcass.

part black (or part Asian, part Native American, etc.) Part white. All other usages are demeaning because they assume white is the standard.

patient (especially when referring to the developmentally or physically inconvenienced). Client; guest.

peddler, sidewalk. Unpremisesed business person.

perfume. Discretionary fragrance. Example: *Rosa was allergic to Bianca's* **discretionary fragrance**, *and demanded that she be removed from the hearing room.*

perverted. Sexually dysfunctional.[59]

pest. Temporarily hostless nonhuman animal who just happens to want to bite, sting, infest, lay eggs in, or suck blood from a human animal.[60]

pet. Companion animal; animal companion; friend; protector.

A **companion animal.**

pet rock. Mineral companion.

pimps. Individuals holding management positions in the sexual work force.[61] See also: prostitutes.

politically correct. Culturally sensitive; multiculturally unexceptionable; appropriately inclusive. The term "politically correct," co-opted by the white power elite as a tool for attacking multiculturalism, is no longer "politically correct."

poor. Economically exploited; economically marginalized; low-income; differently advantaged.

pregnant. Parasitically oppressed.

prison cell. Custody suite.

prisoner. Client of the correctional system; guest in a correctional institution[62]; incarcerated-American. Example : *"I am a self-released* **client of the correctional system,"** *barked Ted, "and either you get me some clothes and some food in a real hurry, or I'll blow your heads off!"*

pro-abortion. Pro-choice.

promiscuous. Sexually active.

prostitutes. Sex care providers; sexual surrogates; sex workers; persons presenting themselves as commodity allotments within a business doctrine.

psychotic. Socially misaligned. See also: **serial killer.**

puppet. Hand-held American.

A **hand-held American** *reading a processed tree carcass.*

Rancher. Cattle murderer.[63]

A **cattle murderer.**

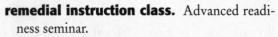

real mother, real father, real parent (of an adopted child). Birthmother, birthfather, birthparent.

remedial instruction. Additional preparation.

remedial instruction class. Advanced readiness seminar.

retard (as a noun). Late developer; chronic underachiever; less prepared individual[64]; mentally challenged person.

riot. Spontaneous display of community dissatisfaction with prevailing socioeconomic conditions.

Sado-masochistic. Differently pleasured.

scholars (specifically, the conservative ones who defend the "canon"). Defined by Mary Daly, in *Gyn/Ecology*, as "abominable snowmen of androcratic academia."[65]

seamstress. Seamstron; or, as Val Dumond helpfully suggests in *The Elements of Nonsexist Usage*, sewer.

second baseman. Second baseperson.

second-homeless. Leisure-residence-deprived.[66]

secretary. Personal assistant.[67]

seducer/seductress. Seductron.

seminal. Ovular.

seminar. Ovarium; ovular (especially when women are among the attendees). Example: *Although participants in the linguistics* *policy* **ovular** *were unable to decide whether "semantics" should be changed to "sefemtics" or "ovulantics," they did vote unanimously to substitute "gaynym" for "homonym."*

senile. Increasingly distracted.

serial killer. Person with difficult-to-meet needs. See also: **psychotic.**

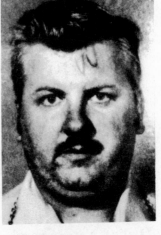

John Wayne Gacy, a **person with difficult-to-meet needs.**

she. Co; tey; ve.

shoplifter. Nontraditional shopper.

short. Vertically challenged; vertically inconvenienced; vertically constrained.

slave. Enslaved person.

sloppy. Nontraditionally ordered; specially organized.

slum. Substandard housing.

snowman. Snowhuman; snowhufem; snow person; person of snow; snow icon.

A **snowhuman.**

spacey. Differently focused.

spendthrift. Negative saver.

spouse. Significant other; partner.

stoned. Chemically inconvenienced.

stupid. Cerebrally challenged; mentally challenged; differently logical.

substitutes. Others. The new term was instituted by Rick Burns, coach of the Mount Holyoke College women's soccer team, after players protested that the word "substitutes" was demeaning to those who just happened to be less skilled.[68]

suffragette. Suffragist.[69] American women, unlike their British sisters, found the label "suffragette" demeaning, and it enjoyed currency only with their political opponents. See: **gender enders** (in Part I).

suicidal. Spiritually dysfunctional.

suicide. Autoeuthanasia; voluntary death.

swapping sex partners. Consensual nonmonogamy.[70]

T

tall. Vertically inconvenienced; vertically challenged.

tempter/temptress. Temptron.

testimony. Ovarimony.

testing, educational. Needs assessment.

third baseman. Third baseperson.

tribe. Nation; people. The term "tribe" should be avoided "whenever possible when referring to Native American peoples," writes Robert B. Moore in "Racist Stereotyping in the English Language," because it "has assumed a connotation of primitiveness or backwardness."[71]

U

ugly. Cosmetically different.

unattractive. See: **ugly.**

underdeveloped. Overexploited.

uneducated. Alternatively schooled.

unemployed. Nonwaged; involuntarily leisured; indefinitely idled; occupationally dispossessed; temporarily outplaced; vocationally deprived; in an orderly transition between career changes.[72]

untrustworthy. Ethically disoriented; morally different; differently honest.

V **vagrant.** Nonspecifically destinationed individual; directionally impoverished person.[73]

vicious (when describing a nonhuman animal). The preferred nonspeciesist term is "differently evolved."

The velociraptor, a **differently evolved** *being.*

victim. Survivor.

W

waiter/waitress. Waitron; waitperson; dining room attendant.

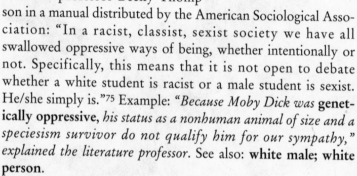

A **waitron.**

washerwoman. Laundron.[74]

white. Melanin impoverished; genetically oppressive (especially when referring to white males). Explains Brandeis professor Becky Thompson in a manual distributed by the American Sociological Association: "In a racist, classist, sexist society we have all swallowed oppressive ways of being, whether intentionally or not. Specifically, this means that it is not open to debate whether a white student is racist or a male student is sexist. He/she simply is."[75] Example: *"Because Moby Dick was* **genetically oppressive,** *his status as a nonhuman animal of size and a speciesism survivor do not qualify him for our sympathy,"* *explained the literature professor.* See also: **white male; white person.**

white male. Racist, sexist. "It is true that not all white men are capitalists or possess extreme class privilege," explains Barbara Smith in "Notes for Yet Another Paper on Black Feminism," "but it is safe to assume that 99.44 percent of them are racists and sexists. It is not just rich and powerful capitalists who destroy life. Rapists, murderers, lynchers and ordinary bigots do too and exercise very real and violent power because of their white-male privilege."[76] See also: **white; white person.**

white person. Ice person; person of noncolor; member of the mutant albino genetic-recessive global minority. "Person of noncolor," we are told in *A Feminist Dictionary,* is especially appropriate to describe white Anglo-Saxon Protestants. See also: **white; white male.**

wife. Significant other; partner; unpaid sex worker; domestic incarceration survivor. In using these terms, Val Dumond warns us in *Elements of Nonsexist Usage*, it is particularly important to avoid possessive terms such as "my significant other," or "my partner." "When two people marry," she writes, "one does not become the property of the other; one does not belong to the other. Likewise, two married people do not become one, implying two half-people. Two married people become two people sharing their lives."[77] Example: *Lot became very upset when the **unpaid sex worker** with whom he had been sharing his life was transformed into a pillar of salt, which was clearly nutritionally undesirable in such large quantities.*

wife-swapping. See: swapping sex partners.

wild. Free-roaming.

wino. Substance abuse survivor; person of stupor; person of differing sobriety.

*A **person of differing sobriety.***

woman. Wofem; womban; womon; womyn; woperson; person of gender.

women. Wimmin; wimyn; womyn. Example: *"A woman is only a woman, but a good cigar is a smoke, which should, of course, be enjoyed only in areas set aside for tobacco users,"* observed Reginald, *whose concern for the health of others was, alas, not matched by a sensitivity to **wimmin's** issues.*

wool. Stolen nonhuman-animal fibers. Example: *"Don't try to pull the **stolen nonhuman-animal fibers** over my eyes!"* said

Rhonda to the ethically disoriented previously-enjoyed-car salesperson.

worst. Least best. A term used by the United Parcel Service in rating its drivers.[78]

wrong. Differently logical. Example: " '2+2=5' isn't wrong, Johnny," Johnny's teacher assured him. "It just happens to be **differently logical.**"

Y

yeti. See: Bigfoot.

Z

zoo. Animalcatraz, zulag,[79] or (as the newly-named NYZS /The Wildlife Conservation Society[80]—formerly the New York Zoological Society—now insists that it be called) wildlife preservation center.

Dr. Seuss, author of the beloved children's classic, If I Ran the **Wildlife Preservation Center.**

zoo keeper; zoo guide. Barbara Rose, writing to *The New York Times Magazine* to commend NYZS/The Wildlife Conservation Society—formerly the New York Zoological Society—on its decision to stop using the term "zoo," explained that those formerly called "zoo keepers" are now more properly referred to as "wildlife friends." The job title "zoo guide," Ms. Rose informed the *Times*, has been changed to "wildlife preservation center docent."[81]

P A R T
T H R E E

OTHER SUSPECT WORDS,
CONCEPTS, AND
"HEROES" TO BE AVOIDED
AND/OR DISCARDED

A **academic freedom.** Harvard professor Barbara Johnson announced, at a symposium held at the university under the acronym AWARE (Actively Working Against Racism and Ethnocentrism), that "professors should have less freedom of expression than writers and artists, because professors are supposed to be creating a better world."[1] See also: **freedom of speech and the First Amendment.**

American flag, display of, in time of war. During the Persian Gulf War, the University of Maryland took the courageous step of requesting that students remove any American flags that happened to be hanging from their windows. "[T]his is a very diverse community, and what may be innocent to one person may be insulting to another," explained university official Jan Davidson. (The university was immediately besieged with predictable arguments such as "the Supreme Court says it's O.K. to burn the flag, so why shouldn't it be all right to display it, too," and, having made its point, retracted its request.)[2]

animals, anthropomorphization of. A group of artists at the University of Illinois demanded that a work by French sculptor Emmanuel Fremiet on display in a local museum—a bronze statue of a gorilla running off with a woman—be melted down on the grounds that such "anthropomorphizing of animals inevitably leads to racist representation." But, the artists were asked, wouldn't destruction of the sculpture be an act of censorship? On the contrary, the artists explained, the meltdown demand was an act of "constructive criticism" which called attention to "the museum's own practice of censorship through exclusion."[3]

animals, domestication of. The domestication of animals is "an unnatural process, a method of enslaving animals and subjecting their life processes to our will," writes noted nonhuman animal activist Harriet Schleifer, cofounder of the Quebec Animal Liberation Collective. Tom Regan, professor of philosophy at North Carolina State University and author of "The Case for Animal Rights," agrees. "To right the wrong of our treatment of farm animals requires more than making rearing methods more humane," he argues. "It requires the total dissolution of commercial animal agriculture....The fate of the animals is in our hands," Regan concludes. "God grant we are equal to the task."[4]

B **the Bering Strait Theory of the settlement of America.** Amylee, author of "How Not to Talk to an Indian," dismisses the theory that the original inhabitants of North America first came to the continent across a land bridge where the Bering Strait is today as a bald attempt by Eurocentric scientists to "justify non-Native invasion by hypothesizing that Natives were once invaders."[5]

bestowal of favors upon women. "[A man's] need to denigrate women may be couched in gratuitous behavior, flattery and the bestowal of favors," reasons Sue Rosenberg Zalk in "Men in the Academy: A Psychological Profile of Harassment." "Although this seems to suggest a fondness for the person, it may well be a vehicle for rendering the woman submissive, dependent and obliged."[6]

the Book of Genesis. The *Book of Genesis*—a patriarchal work if ever there was one—is fatally flawed, according to Mary Daly and other feminist scholars, because it presents Woman as having been born from Man, rather than the other way around (Daly calls this "The Myth of Male Motherhood"), and, worse still, because it blames Woman for tempting Man into evil.[7]

the Book of Genesis, feminist interpretation of. The feminist view of the *Book of Genesis* is fatally flawed, Peter Singer and other animal rights activists imply, because, while it properly chastises the patriarchal authors of the Bible for blaming Woman for helping tempt Man into evil, it fails to note that the serpent—a defenseless nonhuman animal—is even less fairly treated.[8]

clarity. Dinesh D'Souza reports in *Illiberal Education* that some postmodernist literary and social critics write badly *on purpose* "in order, they say, to call language, culture, and learning into question and even bring them into dispute."[9] Fearing, perhaps, that some naïve readers may find this hard to believe, D'Souza offers as proof the following passage from *Saving the Text: Literature/Derrida/Philosophy* by Geoffrey Hartman, a deconstructionist professor at Yale University:

> Because of the equivocal echo-nature of language, even identities or homophones sound on: the sound of Sa is knotted with that of Ça, as if the text were signalling its intention to bring Hegel, Saussure and Freud together. Ça corresponds to the Freudian Id (Es); and it may be that our "savoir absolu" is that of a Ça structured like the Sa-significant: a bacchic or Lacanian "primal process" where only signifier-signifying signifiers exist.[10]

classics, literary. "I get tired of reading the thoughts of white men who would probably spit on me if they were alive to face me today," explains Joseph Green in a landmark article in the *Stanford Daily* entitled "Western Culture is Racist."[11] Besides, adds Professor Stanley Hauerwas of the Duke Divinity School, "the canon of great literature was created by high-Anglican ass----s to underwrite their social class."[12] Indeed, even if "classics" of Eurocentric literature were not oppressive in content, granting them a "privileged" place in the literary canon would violate the central precept of such modern literary theories as deconstructionism and reader-response criticism that no work is inherently more valuable than any other.

"conspicuous exclusion of students from conversations," legality of. See: freedom of speech and the First Amendment.

Constitution, American. A report by a New York State Board of Education task force (1989) condemned the Constitution as "the embodiment of the White Male with Property Model." Professor Houston Baker of the University of Pennsylvania dismissed it at a symposium at Yale's Whitney Humanities Center as a "gothic romance."[13]

creativity. See originality.

D **dating.** As National Book Award–winning poet Adrienne Rich has pointed out, the white male dominant culture depends upon "compulsory heterosexuality" to retain "physical, economical, and emotional access" to women. When a woman accepts an invitation to dinner or a movie, therefore, she is willingly submitting to the continued subjugation of herself and her gender. The supposed "interest" which "boys and girls are supposed to show" in dating during their teenage years, Rich concludes, is only a consequence of phallocentric social conditioning.[14]

daycare centers. Institutions that, in the words of Shulamith Firestone, "buy women off. They ease the immediate pressure without asking why that pressure is on *women.*"[15]

E **English, standard.** Steve Parks of the University of Pennsylvania, a speaker at the Fourth National Basic Writing Conference held at the University of Maryland in late 1992, announced that standard English was the language of the slavemasters, and applauded African-Americans for resisting it. "It is not *their* language that is subject to error and needs change," he said, during a general dismissal of basic writing courses, "it is *our* approach."[16]

F
facts. See: reality.

family, nuclear. Allison Jaggar, a professor at the University of Cincinnati and the chairperson of the Committee on the Status of Women in Philosophy of the American Philosophical Association, points out that the nuclear family is "the cornerstone of women's oppression" because it "enforces heterosexuality" and "imposes the prevailing masculine and feminine character structures on the next generation."[17]

fifties nostalgia. Dean Hilda Hernandez-Graeville of Harvard suggested that the university ban fifties nostalgia parties because racism was particularly rampant in America during that particular time period.[18]

flash cameras. On the grounds that the majority who happen not to have epilepsy have no right to impose intermittent flashes of light on those who might experience a seizure as a result, the first National Lesbian Conference in Atlanta, Georgia, officially declared its proceedings flash-camera-free.[19]

freedom of speech and the First Amendment. In a landmark victory for the new fairness over the abstract concept of "free speech," which the forces of oppression have traditionally used as a smoke screen to hide their opposition to diversity, the University of Connecticut recently issued an official ban on **inappropriately directed laughter** and the **conspicuous exclusion of students from conversations.** Despite the fact that *not one witness* came forward to argue in favor of inappropriately directed laughter or conspicuous exclusion of students from conversations, the ban was declared "unconstitutional" and rescinded. That such setbacks are merely temporary, however, is demonstrated by President George Bush's courageous November 1991 veto of Congress's attempt to allow personnel in the federally-funded health clinic hierarchy to impose their views on low-income women.[20]

French, Russian, and Italian salad dressings, unprotesting acceptance of by African-Americans. In the revised edition of *Afrocentricity,* Molefi Kete Asante argues persuasively that by responding "French," "Russian," or "Italian," to the question "What kind of salad dressing do you prefer?" African-Americans are "participating subconsciously in the drama of Europe." However, Asante notes, since the publication of the first edition of his book, there have been some positive developments. "[W]e now have dressings with names like Ghanian, Nigerian, Senegalese and Tanzanian," he writes. "The idea is that the Afrocentrist refuses to be inundated by a symbolic reality which denies her existence."[21]

G**ettysburg Address.** Mary Daly, of the Boston College Department of Theology, cites it as a prototypical example of "bull."[22] Lincoln's phallocratic words, she points out, condemn themselves: "Fourscore and seven years ago our fathers brought forth upon this continent a new nation, conceived in liberty, and dedicated to the proposition that all men are created equal."

Abraham Lincoln delivering the **Gettysburg Address.**

Goya's "The Naked Maja." A reproduction of Francisco de Goya's painting "The Naked Maja" was banished from the wall of a classroom at Penn State University's Schuylkill campus after English instructor Nancy Stumhofer called attention to the pivotal role the work had played in the creation of a hostile environment for faculty and students. "Any nude picture of a female," she noted, "encourages males to make remarks about body parts." The offending work had hung in the classroom for ten years, reports *U.S. News & World Report* columnist John Leo, "before it began harassing Stumhofer."[23]

*Francisco de Goya's "***The Naked Maja.***"*

grammar. "'Proper grammar,'" writes noted Canadian language reformer Betsy Warland, "like 'proper manners,' shields us from the raw material of what is going on. Black women writers have been circumventing this ethnocentric white patriarchal structuring of language (and consequently thought itself) for years. Walter Ong, in his book *Interfaces of the Word*, sheds light on the results of this disparity: 'With writing, the earlier noetic state (primary orality) undergoes a kind of cleavage, separating the knower from the external universe and then from himself.'"[24]

H **Halloween parties.** The majority faction of the Student Senate of the University of Wisconsin at Madison voted down a proposal for an all-campus masquerade ball on the grounds that people wearing masks can take advantage of their anonymity to inflict "poking, pinching, rude comments," etc., on women and members of other traditionally oppressed groups.[25]

handshakes. As Nancy Henley explains in *Body Politics*, the handshake is "a masculine ritual of recognition and affirmation" which "serves to perpetuate male clubbiness and to exclude women from the club."[26]

A **handshake.**

"inappropriately directed laughter," legality of. See: freedom of speech and the First Amendment.

individual liberties. When a student at the University of Pennsylvania wrote her colleagues on the school's Diversity Education Committee, informing them of her "deep regard for the individual" and her "desire to protect the freedoms of all members of society," a helpful college administrator returned her letter with the word "individual" underlined. "This is a 'RED FLAG' phrase today which many consider RACIST," he advised her. "Arguments that champion the individual over the group ultimately privilege the 'INDIVIDUALS' belonging to the largest or dominant group."[27]

intercourse, heterosexual. "Coitus," Andrea Dworkin informs us, "is punishment."[28]

Ivy League colleges. According to Gregory Ricks, a former dean at Dartmouth, Ivy League schools "might be the slickest form of genocide going"—at least with respect to "blacks, feminists, and others trying to change the status quo." To prove his point he told a Harvard racial sensitivity seminar about an African-American student who, in high school, "had visions of kicking the world's ass," but no longer felt he was up to it, thanks to a Dartmouth "education" that "turned [him] around and fucked up [his] mind."[29]

Jefferson, Thomas. Harvard Afro-American Studies majors Tiya Miles, Eva Nelson, and Michelle Duncan described Jefferson, during the course of an interview with Dinesh D'Souza, as a

Thomas Jefferson.

"hypocrite," a "total racist," and "a rapist." Nelson added that Abraham Lincoln was "a joke...a mess," offering as proof the fact that Lincoln had said that "if he could save the union without freeing the slaves, he would do it."[30] (Note: These opinions carry particular weight because of the unusual academic background that interviewer D'Souza brings to any discussion of racism. The former White House domestic policy analyst was a staffer on the *Dartmouth Review* when the magazine illustrated an interview with a former KKK leader by staging a photo of an African-American strung up from a tree on the Dartmouth campus, and when it held a free lobster-and-champagne banquet to celebrate a campuswide fast designed to call attention to world hunger.[31])

leaflets, handing out. The first National Lesbian Conference in Atlanta, Georgia, officially banned the handing out of leaflets to its delegates on the grounds that the practice is "inherently coercive." Leafleting, a spokesperson for the conference explained, puts "the woman you're handing something to in a position where she has to say no, and everyone knows how difficult it is in this culture to say no."[32]

Lincoln, Abraham. See: Gettysburg Address; Jefferson, Thomas.

literate cultures, inherent superiority of. Amoja Three Rivers reminds us, in *Cultural Etiquette: A Guide for the Well-Intentioned*, that the spoken word offers a "more immediate and personal communication and transmission of culture" than the written one and, for this reason among others, cultures based on the oral tradition are "just as 'good' and 'smart'" as literate ones. Thinking of nonliterate cultures as "backward," she adds, is simply closing one's mind to "a world-view that differs from that of the 20th century European."[33]

M **male door-opening ritual.** A cynical symbol of patriarchal subjugation. In her essay "Oppression," philosopher Marilyn Frye explains: "[T]he message is that women are incapable. The detachment of the acts from the concrete realities of what women need and do not need is a vehicle for the message that women's actual needs and interests are unimportant or irrelevant. Finally, these gestures imitate the behavior of servants toward masters and thus mock women, who are in most respects the servants and caretakers of men. The message of the false helpfulness of male gallantry is female dependence, the invisibility or insignificance of women, and contempt for women."[34]

male sexuality. "The ethics of male sexuality are essentially rapist," John Stollenberg informs us in *Refusing to Be a Man*. "The idea of the male sex is like the idea of an Aryan race....It is a political entity that flourishes only through acts of force and sexual terrorism."[35]

marriage. Andrea Dworkin defines marriage as a legal contract which sanctions rape. Even worse, she notes, it give the husband/rapist *exclusive* rights to rape the woman whom he marries: any "second rapist" who happens to come along is immediately condemned as "an adulterer." (Dr. Dale Spender takes a slightly less negative view of marriage, seeing it not as "rape" but merely as legalized prostitution—the exchange of sexual services for "support.")[36]

meaning. According to deconstructionist theory, all meaning is "socially constructed." In other words, no statement or word—including the word "meaning"—has any intrinsic meaning. It follows, therefore, that no tools exist to disprove this theory, and that anyone who attempts to do so is not only logocentric, but also suffers from the delusion of false consciousness.

men and women, difference between. See: women and men, difference between.

Middle East. An artificial construct of Eurocentric nineteenth century geographers who, willing to go to any length to avoid the unpleasant admission that Africans built the pyramids and the Sphinx, found a way of "stealing" Egypt from the continent in which any map clearly shows it belongs.[37]

Milton, John. A Duke University English major informed author Dinesh D'Souza he "wouldn't touch Milton" because "I know what the guy was up to—he was a sexist through and through."[38]

John Milton.

Opposing, in court, the case of a member of a traditionally underrepresented group. When the moot court board of the New York University Law School tried to assign a case on the custody rights of a lesbian mother, culturally sensitive students successfully forced them to withdraw it, on the grounds that "writing arguments [against the mother's side] is hurtful to a group of people and thus hurtful to all of us."[39]

originality. According to the catalog of the Whitney Museum's 1993 Biennial Exhibition, the emerging generation of artists has deliberately rejected "originality" on the grounds that it is one of the "emblems" of what the predominantly white, male, heterosexual art world deems "successful art." "To the highminded," the catalog points out, these new works might appear "defeatist or inept. But that is the point."[40]

Parenthood, biological. Ann Ferguson, in "Androgyny as an Ideal for Human Development," tells us that biological parenthood must be deemphasized in favor of communal living in order to "eliminate the subordination of women in the patriarchal nuclear family" and to "allow homosexuals and bisexuals the opportunity to have an equal part in relating to children."[41]

"past life regression" as a means of entering someone else's identity group. In "Just Don't Do This, Okay?," a chapter of her pamphlet *Cultural Etiquette: A Guide for the Well-Intentioned*, Amoja Three Rivers—apparently speaking from experience—specifically warns white people not to "go round expecting you can be part of another ethnic group now because you feel you were of that group in a former life."[42]

phrases that contain words that, in another context, have been used oppressively. *Time* magazine reports that an administrator at the University of California at Santa Cruz has campaigned for the banning of such phrases as "a nip in the air" and "a chink in his armor" on the grounds that they contain words that, in other contexts, have been used to express prejudice.[43]

prose. A form of expression that, because it is not equally available to all social and economic classes, is inherently oppressive. Audre Lorde, the late African-American lesbian feminist-socialist, is particularly illuminating on this issue in her essay "Age, Race, Class and Sex: Women Redefining Difference." "We need to be aware," she points out, that "reams of paper...a typewriter...plenty of time...[and] a room of one's own," may be "a necessity" for writing prose, and that the creation of such art is therefore more and more the exclusive province of the privileged classes. Similarly, she adds, "the actual requirements to produce the visual arts...help determine, along class lines, whose art is whose." Poetry, on the other hand, is "the most economical" form our creativity can take. It is "the most secret," "the least material," and "can be done between shifts, in the hospital pantry, on the subway and on scraps of surplus paper." Thus, she concludes, poetry—not prose or the visual arts—is the medium of choice as "we reclaim our literature."[44]

R **reading.** Houston Baker, Jr., professor of human relations at the University of Pennsylvania, has declared that "reading and writing are merely technologies of control. [They are] martial law made academic."[45] In 1991, perhaps on the strength of insights such as this, Baker assumed the presidency of the Modern Language Association.

reality. Postmodernist techniques of analysis, such as deconstructionism and antifoundationalism, have demonstrated that there is no objective reality. Any argument which *appears* to be grounded on "universal principles," postmodernists will tell you, mistakenly assumes the validity of its own truth claims; in other words, it is a product of circular reasoning based entirely on the arguer's artificially constructed belief system. "Questions of fact, truth, correctness, validity, and clarity can neither be posed nor answered," explains Duke professor Stanley Fish, with characteristic succinctness (if not clarity).[46] See also: **clarity; meaning.**

responding to the sexual advances of a woman less powerful than oneself. Sue Rosenberg Zalk, the director of the Center for the Study of Women and Society at the State University of New York, notes that a woman who successfully seduces a man who outranks her in a hierarchy is a victim of "sexist oppression." The "unequal power relationship" between them means that the man—or "receptive noninitiator," as Zalk labels the offender in such cases—is still taking unfair advantage of the woman. Indeed, waiting for her to make the first move, rather than inviting sexual contact himself, puts the man "in the position to give or not give what is requested of him," thereby actually *increasing* his power and control over his victim. Why then is such behavior not more widely condemned? "In our society a woman's offer of free sex is considered a logical explanation for a man's indulgence," Zalk tells us. "The stereotype about men's pervasive sexual needs and dominating drive to satisfy them prevail to the degree that we consider such behavior normal, or at least understandable."[47]

scientific inquiry. A New Jersey state-sponsored task force charged with finding ways to eliminate sexist bias in the teaching of college-level science discovered that what we've always known as scientific procedure is merely a patriarchal conspiracy. "[M]ind was male," the group concluded. "Nature was female, and knowledge was created as an act of aggression—a passive nature had to be interrogated, unclothed, penetrated, and compelled by man to reveal her secrets."[48]

standards, for good writing. Tom Fox, the director of a writing program at California State University, Chico, noted, at the Fourth National Basic Writing Conference held at the University of Maryland in autumn, 1992, that a concern for traditional standards is the hobbyhorse of reactionaries. If he were forced to offer standards of his own, he added, they would be these: good writing must "be relentlessly plural," "interrogate political inequities," and "oppose homophobia."[49]

staring, legality of. In a landmark sexual harassment decision, Richard Hummel, a chemical engineering professor at the University of Toronto, was convicted of "prolonged and intense staring" while swimming in a campus pool. Hummel is unlikely to repeat the offense: the case cost him more than $200,000 in charges and fees.[50]

Terms of endearment. In its *Dictionary of Cautionary Words and Phrases,* a list of words offered as "a guide to alert journalists that certain words and phrases are simply unacceptable," the 1989 Multicultural Management Program Fellows [sic] of the University of Missouri Journalism School note that several "terms of endearment" are to be avoided because men have traditionally used them to belittle or trivialize women. Three words they single out as particularly objectionable are "dear" (especially in such phrases as "She is a dear"), "sweetie," and "honey."[51]

tolerance of the nonoppressed. "Tolerance is a loaded virtue," says Gayatri Spivak, professor of English and cultural studies at Pittsburgh University, "because you have to have a base of power to practice it. You cannot ask a certain people to 'tolerate' a culture that has historically ignored them, at the same time that their children are being indoctrinated into it."[52]

truth. See: reality.

"trying to pass" as nonvictimized. Mary P. Koss, professor of psychiatry at the University of Arizona and author of the famous Koss Report on date rape, reports that a persistent obstacle to the elimination of sexual oppression from campus life is victims' "trying to pass as nonvictimized."[53]

the two-sexes concept. Brown University geneticist and intersexual-rights advocate Anne Fausto-Sterling argues convincingly that the conventional Western belief that there are only two sexes—male and female—is an oppressive political construct which flies in the face of natural evidence. Writes Fausto-Sterling: "There are many gradations running from female to male; along that spectrum lie at least five sexes—perhaps even more."[54]

Victims of the *Challenger* disaster, sympathy for. Leonard Jeffries, chairman of the Afro-American Studies Department of the City University of New York, has been quoted as saying that the destruction of the *Challenger* should be applauded because it deterred white people from "spreading their filth throughout the universe."[55]

visual arts. See: prose.

voice, active. Because it attaches "excessive importance to the capacities of a single individual to effect change,"[56] and because it champions self-interest over the broader interests of one's community as a whole, the active voice is, as New York media critic Josh Ozersky has pointed out, deeply suspect within the multicultural movement. Ozersky offers as an example of "distasteful" usage the sentence "I do not see this as a sexist text." A more "enlightened" version would be: "It is seen as a sexist text, by some."[57] See: **voice, passive.**

voice, passive. Because it permits oppressors to "obscure relationships and erase responsibility,"[58] the passive voice is deeply suspect within the multicultural movement. For example, as linguist Julia Penelope Stanley has written, the statement "Mary was abused as a child" obscures the fact that she was abused by *her father.*[59] See: **voice, active.**

Women and men, difference between. Using as evidence the story of a seventeenth century French hermaphrodite, the celebrated literary critic Stephen Greenblatt argues forcefully, in an essay called "Fiction and Friction," that sexual difference is "unstable and artificial."[60]

words derived from Greek or Latin. In *Language, Gender and Professional Writing,* Francine Wattman Frank and Paula A. Treichler note a trend among feminists, traceable to "Virginia Woolf's day," to resist words derived from Greek or Latin, based on the fact that these languages can "be seen as accoutrements of male privilege." Such resistance is, of course, perfectly understandable, Frank and Treichler point out, since "any term may come to be seen as problematic after its etymology and other associations are articulated in contemporary discourse." Nonetheless, they add, the flight from Greek and Latin is not without irony, since these languages were "denounced in earlier centuries as feminizing influences that threatened to destroy the robust masculinity of Anglo-Saxon English."[61]

words that equate bad, depressing, or negative things with darkness. It is offensive, Amoja Three Rivers advises us in *Cultural Etiquette: A Guide for the Well-Intentioned,* to use words and phrases such as "a black mood," a "dark day," and "a black heart" that "equate bad, depressing, or negative things with darkness." "Be creative," she suggests. "There are thousands of adjectives in the English language that do not equate evil with the way people of color look. How about instead of 'the pot calling the kettle black' you say 'the pus calling the maggot white'?"[62]

writing. See: reading.

writing about communities of which one is not a member. *Ms.* magazine has made it official policy that every article it publishes on the subject of lesbians must be written by a lesbian.[63]

P A R T
F O U R

KNOW YOUR OPPRESSOR

A Bilingual Glossary
of
Bureaucratically Suitable (BS)
Language

BUREAUCRATICALLY SUITABLE/ BUREAUCRATICALLY UNSUITABLE

The following is a concise dictionary of terminology considered appropriate for use in corporate and government circles.

A **above critical.** Out of control and in danger of melting down (when referring to a nuclear reactor).[1] Example: *"Whoopsy daisy," remarked the plant operator, "I think this baby is a teensy bit* **above critical,** *and we could be seeing some core rearrangement here."* See also: **core rearrangement; event; superprompt critical power excursion.**

acceptable. Unacceptable—except to those using the term. Consider, for example, the phrase "acceptable unemployment," which, as language expert Paul Dickson has written, means "acceptable to those who have a job."[2]

accidental delivery of ordnance equipment. Bombing something other than the intended target—a civilian hospital, for example, or one's own troops.[3] See also: **friendly fire; incontinent ordnance.**

acquiescent volunteers. The British government's term for Vietnamese refugees forcibly returned to Vietnam from Hong Kong.

aggressive defense. U.S. military term for an aggressive offensive attack.[4] See also: **preemptive counterattack.**

air support. Bombing.[5] See also: **armed reconnaissance; terrain alteration.**

anomaly. Accident. After the space shuttle *Challenger* blew up, for example, NASA spokesperson Kay Parker announced that flight simulators were being used in the course of "the anomaly investigation."[6]

A space vehicle **anomaly.**

arbitrary deprivation of life. Murder. A 1984 term designated for use in U.S. State Department reports describing friendly governments such as those in El Salvador and Chile, because, as Assistant Secretary of State Elliott Abrams put it, "we found the term 'killing' too broad."[7]

armed reconnaissance. Bombing.[8] See also: **air support; terrain alteration.**

atmospheric deposition of anthropogenically derived acidic substances. Acid rain.[9] See also: **poorly buffered precipitation.**

aversion therapy. Shock treatment; torture.[10]

Aversion therapy.

B bio-robot. A man dispatched to do work so dangerous it was originally intended to be performed only by mechanical devices. The term was coined by the Soviet managers of the Chernobyl clean-up.[11]

career alternative enhancement program. What the Chrysler Corporation "initiated" when it eliminated five thousand jobs at its American Motors plant in Kenosha, Wisconsin.[12] Example: *"Clean out your desk and hit the bricks, toots,"* said Ms. Jones's supervisor as he handed her a pink slip. "We're initiating a* **career alternative enhancement program** *tailored specifically for you."*

career-change opportunity. A phrase used by a Vermont corporation to explain why its dismissal of fifteen employees was "not a cutback or a layoff."[13]

categorical inaccuracy. Lie.[14]

collateral damage. Civilian deaths or injuries, and/or the destruction of civilian property, caused by a military attack.[15]

compliance assistance officers. U.S. Environmental Protection Agency's term for its enforcement personnel.[16]

contributions. Tax payments. The term became popular during the early days of the Clinton administration.[17] See also: **sacrifices.**

controlled flight into terrain. An airplane crash.[18] See also: **failure to maintain clearance from the ground.**

Controlled flight into terrain.

core rearrangement. The explosive destruction of the core of a nuclear reactor.[19] See also: **above critical; event; superprompt critical power excursion.**

Reactor building at Chernobyl, April 26, 1986, showing the side effects of a **core rearrangement event.**

counterfactual proposition. Lie.[20] Example: *Todd's favorite bureaucratically suitable film was sex,* **counterfactual propositions,** *and videotape.*

crew transfer containers. The coffins of pilots or astronauts who have been rendered nonviable by an anomaly or by hostile or incontinent ordnance.[21]

D

decruit. Fire.[22]

deep ocean placement. Dumping wastes in the ocean.[23]

deferred maintenance.

Failure to paint, clean, or perform required minor repairs on a building, machine, or vehicle.[24] Example: *The structural integrity of the Colosseum in Rome has been disenhanced by nearly 1,500 years of* **deferred maintenance.** See: **substantial deferred maintenance.**

The Roman Colosseum, after 15 centuries of **deferred maintenance.**

depopulation. The U.S. government's term for the gassing of 7 million chickens in Pennsylvania in 1983, an effort designed to help contain an outbreak of influenza.[25] See also: **harvesting; wildlife management.**

diagnostic misadventure of high magnitude. Accidental death of a hospital patient caused by malpractice during the examination process.[26] An accidental death caused by the treatment itself is known as a **therapeutic misadventure.**[27]

directive improvement. Discipline.[28] Example: *When it became clear that* **directive improvement** *had not positively affected his performance, Hugo was asked to take early retirement.*

disengaged. See: hands-off management style.

downsizing. Laying off or firing a significant percentage of one's employees.[29] It should be noted, however, that in its March 19, 1991, edition, *The Wall Street Journal* reported that the term "downsizing" was being quickly replaced in business usage by the more positive words **rightsizing** and **streamlining**.[30] See also: reduction activities; restructuring; strategic downsizing; redundancy elimination.

E **early stages of finalization, in the.** Unfinished. Once 50 percent of a project has been completed, it may be characterized as "semifinalized."[31]

energetic disassembly. An explosion, especially an accidental one.[32] Example: *The* **energetic disassembly** *of the zeppelin* Hindenburg *has left plans for lighter-than-air passenger travel in the early stages of finalization for more than half a century.*

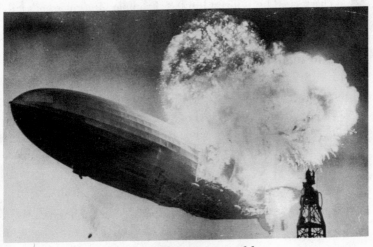

An **energetic disassembly.**

engage the enemy on all sides. Get ambushed (as defined by the U.S. Department of Defense).[33]

equity retreat. Stock market crash.[34] Example: *After the Great Equity Retreat of 1929, a number of stockbrokers took advantage of career-change opportunities to reposition themselves in the apple-marketing field.*

event. An accident, especially a nuclear one.[35] See also: **above critical; core rearrangement; superprompt critical power excursion.**

executive action. A CIA term that lexicographer Hugh Rawson defines as "getting rid of people, especially the leaders of foreign countries, and especially by murder."[36]

exfiltration. Retreat.[37] Example: *Napoleon's exfiltration from Moscow resulted in 470,000 of his 500,000 troops becoming nonviable.* See also: **strategic withdrawal.**

F **failure to fulfill one's wellness potential.** Death (notation made by a physician on a deceased patient's hospital chart, cited by William Lutz).[38] Example: *Andy Warhol's failure to fulfill his wellness potential resulted in a lawsuit against the hospital that treated him.*

failure to maintain clearance from the ground. An airplane crash.[39] See also: **controlled flight into terrain.**

festival seating. No seats—bring a blanket and hope for the best. As Hugh Rawson has pointed out, "it was holders of festival seating tickets who stampeded while trying to get into a rock concert in Cincinnati, Ohio, in 1979, killing eleven people and injuring at least eight more."[40]

force package. One or more warplanes or bombers.[41]

forest management. Killing trees, especially on public lands.[42]

for your convenience. For *our* convenience.[43] Example: **For your convenience,** *kindly check your packages at the courtesy desk.*

friendly fire. An inadvertent attack on one's own troops.[44] See: accidental delivery of ordnance equipment; incontinent ordnance.

Game management. The hunting or mass slaughter of wild animals.[45] Example: *The* game management *of the passenger pigeon during the 19th century was 100 percent effective.*

The passenger pigeon, a paragon of successful **game management.**

good-natured grunts. A term for "booing and hissing," coined by David Beckwith, then vice president Dan Quayle's press secretary, to describe the reaction his boss received from cadets at the U.S. Military Academy when the subject of Quayle's service in the Indiana National Guard during the Vietnam War came up.[46]

good-neighbor policy. Invading a neighboring country. For example, George Will wrote of the U.S. incursion in Panama that "this intervention is a good-neighbor policy. America's role in Panama—in effect, administering a recount on last May's elections—is an act of hemispheric hygiene...."[47] Example: "¡Caramba!" *shouted the National Guard major as American paratroopers began landing in Panama City,* "twenty thousand of our **good neighbors** *have decided to pay us an unexpected visit.*"

great restraint. What police officers always exercise up until the moment they are forced to shoot someone.[48]

H **hands-off management style.** A term used to describe President Ronald Reagan's approach to the Presidency. John Leo defines it as "out to lunch."[49] Example: *Louis XVI's and Marie Antoinette's* **hands-off management style** *was a major factor in their being rendered nonviable.* Also: **disengaged; prefers to leave details to others.**

harvesting. The large-scale killing of trees or animals.[50] See also: **depopulation; wildlife management.**

health alteration. Murder, as defined by the CIA, who, according to writer David Wise, refers to its assassination unit as the "health alteration committee."[51]

I **"I don't doubt your word."** A phrase used by banks, airlines, and retail establishments which, roughly translated, means: "You're probably telling the truth, but so what?" Enid Nemy offers the following example: "**We don't doubt your word** *you reconfirmed your ticket, but it isn't in the computer.*" "Don't bother asking," advises Nemy, "you aren't on the flight."[52]

illiquid. Insolvent. The term was coined by the California Historical Society to describe the situation it found itself in after a decade of multi-hundred-thousand-dollar deficits.[53]

inappropriate behavior. White collar crime, especially after it has been detected.[54] See also: **judgmental lapse.**

inappropriate physical abuse. Police brutality, for example.[55]

incontinent ordnance. Bombs, missiles, or artillery shells that fall on one's own position.[56] See also: **accidental delivery of ordnance equipment; friendly fire.**

indefinitely idle. To lay off an employee.[57]

inoperative statement. Lie. The term was coined by President Richard Nixon's press secretary, Ron Ziegler, who, when confronted with the fact that one of his pronouncements about the Watergate affair appeared to contradict previous "information" on the subject, declared, "This is the operative statement. The others are inoperative."[58]

institutional flexibility. The authority of educational administrators to do anything they want without consulting the faculty as to the effect their actions might have on the quality of education offered by their school.[59]

institutional self-help. Cutting salaries or laying off workers to improve profits.[60]

interdictional nonsuccumbers. Enemy troops who survive a bombing attack.[61] Example: **Interdictional nonsuccumbers** *are always excellent candidates for force-package site revisitation.*

investments. The Clinton administration's term for "government spending."[62]

involuntary conversion. An accidental fire, explosion, collision, or any other "act of God" that "converts" a piece of property from its original state into a pile of rubble. For example, when National Airlines received a $1.7 million insurance payment after the crash of one of its planes, it announced in its annual report that it had received the money as the result of "the involuntary conversion of a 727."[63]

J judgmental lapse. A white collar crime, especially when it involves a course of conduct.[64] Example: *With the benefit of hindsight, BCCI's defrauding its depositors out of billions of dollars might be considered a serious* **judgmental lapse.** See also: **inappropriate behavior.**

L **legislative leadership advocate.** Lobbyist.[65] Example: Legislative leadership advocates *working for the NRA have been remarkably effective in preserving the right of Americans to alter the health of their fellow citizens with automatic weapons.*

M **manage one's staff resources.** A term used by the Sun Oil Company when it involuntarily removed five hundred employees. "We don't characterize it as a lay-off," said a Sun spokesperson at the time. "We're managing our staff resources. Sometimes you manage them up, and sometimes you manage them down."[66]

meaningful downturn. Recession. See also: **period of negative economic growth.**

morally plausible. A phrase describing a policy that seems good and right but is too overt to be carried out inasmuch as it violates the law. William Bennett, for example, when he was America's "drug czar," suggested that beheading convicted drug dealers was "morally plausible," if "legally difficult."[67]

N **negative cash flow.** Losses.[68]

negative deficit. A profit, especially one earned by an institution such as a school or foundation that is not authorized to do so.[69]

negative employee retention. The policy of firing or laying off a portion of a company's work force.[70]

negative patient care outcome. Death (in a hospital).[71] See also: **terminal episode.**

neutralize. Kill or character-assassinate.[72]

no longer a factor. Dead, wounded, or destroyed.[73]

noncertified worker. A substitute worker hired for the purpose of breaking a strike; a scab.[74]

nonfacile handling of newborn. Hospitalese for a doctor or nurse's dropping of a baby at delivery.[75]

nonminority impacted. White only. A term, coined by the Beaumont (Texas) Housing Authority, that has proved especially useful to realtors.[76]

nonperforming asset. A bad loan, for example.[77]

nonrenew. To lay off, fire.[78] Example: *Professor Hill claimed she permitted her employer to sexually harass her because she believed he would* **nonrenew** *her if she didn't.*

nonviable. Dead.[79] See: **no longer a factor.**

not necessarily unconstitutional. Wrong, but the rules don't cover the offense.[80]

O	**organic biomass.** Sewage sludge.[81] See also: **regulated organic nutrients.**

outplacement. Termination of employment.[82]

P	**period of economic adjustment.** Recession; depression.[83]

period of negative economic growth. Recession; depression.[84] See also: **meaningful downturn.**

policy guidelines. Orders.[85]

poorly buffered precipitation. Acid rain.[86] See also: **atmospheric deposition of anthropogenically derived acidic substances.**

preemptive counterattack. Pentagonese for "our troops attacked first."[87] See also: **aggressive defense; preemptive strike.**

preemptive strike. Pentagonese for a sneak bombing attack.[88] Example: *The Japanese refused to apologize for their* **preemptive strike** *on Pearl Harbor after President Bush declined to express regret for the nuclear alteration of terrain in and around Hiroshima and Nagasaki.* See also: **preemptive counterattack.**

prefers to leave details to others. See: hands-off management style.

previously enjoyed. Used; second-hand.

procedural safeguards. Red tape.[89]

pro-life. Antiabortion.

putative offender. Chief Justice William Rehnquist's term for an individual accused of a crime and held without bail before his or her trial on the grounds of "dangerousness." As Professor William Lutz of Rutgers University has pointed out, putative offenders are effectively "judged guilty until proven innocent."[90]

Q **quota.** Any "artificial" means of adjusting racial, ethnic, gender, or cultural balance in American society, except for the privileged consideration the children of prominent European-American alumni receive when applying for college.

R

rapid oxidation. An unfortunate or embarrassing fire.[91] See also: **involuntary conversion.**

Ms. O'Leary's bovine companion animal kicks off the **Rapid Oxidation** *of Chicago, 1871.*

reduced state of awareness, in a. Asleep, drunk, or stoned, especially when the condition results in an accident. The term was popularized by two railroad engineers who used it in the course of explaining how their train managed to jump its tracks after going over seventy miles per hour through a twenty-five m.p.h. zone, causing $1.7 million worth of damage.[92]

reduction activities. Eliminating workers from one's payroll.[93]

redundancy of human resources. Too many employees, a situation that usually leads to **redundancy elimination.**[94]

redundancy elimination. Laying off or firing workers.[95] See: **redundancy of human resources.**

regulated organic nutrients. Sewage sludge.[96] See also: **organic biomass.**

research in retrospect. The creation of a false paper trail of back-dated or altered documents to provide a plausible rationale for investments that were actually made on the basis of illegally obtained inside information.[97]

revenue enhancement. The Reagan administration's preferred term for "tax increase."[98] See **sacrifices; tax base broadening.**

revenue shortfall. Deficit.[99]

reverse engineering. Stealing a design by taking a product apart, seeing how it's made, and copying it.[100]

rightsizing. A more positive term for **downsizing,** i.e., firing or laying off a significant percentage of one's work force.[101] See also: **reduction activities; redundancy elimination; restructuring; streamlining; strategic downsizing.**

right-to-work laws. "Union-busting" legislation, specifically designed to deny workers the right to the fruits of collective bargaining.[102]

S **sacrifices.** A term used by President Bill Clinton to describe increased tax payments.[103] See also: **contributions; revenue enhancement, tax base broadening.**

sanitize. To remove incriminating evidence from; specifically, to edit surreptitiously from a document any material that might subject its author to embarrassment or prosecution.[104]

security assistance. Arms sales.[105]

selected out. Fired.[106]

selective strike. A term for bombing designed to produce, in the words of lexicographer Hugh Rawson, "something less than total annihilation."[107]

semifinalized. See: **early stages of finalization.**

sensitive. Secret, and, most likely, wrong and illegal. For example, John Dean tells us, in *Blind Ambition*, that he used the term "sensitive matter" to refer to his knowledge that his White House colleague Charles Colson was planning to firebomb the Brookings Institution.[108]

service a target. Drop bombs on something or somebody.[109]

Hiroshima, August 6, 1945, shortly after being **serviced** *by a force package.*

skill-mix adjustment. The laying off of employees.[110]

single-use. Disposable, especially when the disposing might be damaging to the environment.[111]

so-called beaches. A term useful when one needs to refer to coastal regions that just happen to have been befouled by one's own company. The Exxon Corporation, for example, whose supertanker the *Exxon Valdez* ran aground in Alaska's Prince William Sound in 1989, described the thirty-five miles of shoreline ravaged by the resultant spill as "so-called beaches, mainly piles of dark, volcanic rock."[112]

soft ordnance. Antipersonnel weapons, such as napalm—so called because they are designed for use against **soft targets**.[113]

soft targets. Humans, or groups of humans, selected to be bombed or otherwise militarily attacked. (By contrast, "hard targets" are buildings, cities, gun emplacements, or other nonorganic structures.)[114]

strategic downsizing. See: downsizing.

strategic misrepresentation. Harvard Business School term for the tactic of hiding facts, bluffing or lying during a business negotiation.[115]

strategic withdrawal. Retreat.[116] See also: **exfiltration.**

streamlining. Laying off or firing a substantial number of employees.[117] See also: **downsizing; strategic downsizing; rightsizing; redundancy elimination; restructuring.**

subholocaust engagement. A relatively benign nuclear conflict; a nuclear war on a scale insufficient to destroy all life on the earth.[118]

suboptimal. Lousy.[119] Example: *Its triumphal launch from Southampton notwithstanding, the* Titanic's *maiden voyage must be considered a* **suboptimal** *transatlantic crossing.*

substandard housing unit. Slum.[120]

substantial deferred maintenance. Failure to perform required major repairs on a building, machine, or vehicle.[121] See: **deferred maintenance.**

superprompt critical power excursion. Nuclear meltdown. The word "excursion" refers to the "runaway" nature of the event.[122] See also: **above critical; core rearrangement; event.**

Tax base broadening. A tax increase.[123] See also: **revenue enhancement; sacrifices.**

tax credit. A Clinton administration term for "tax break."[124]

temporary cessation of hostilities. Peace, as defined by the U.S. Defense Department.[125]

temporary interruption of an economic expansion. A recession. The term was coined by then president George Bush, who proclaimed in his 1991 State of the Union address that "the largest peacetime economic expansion in history has been temporarily interrupted."[126]

terminal episode. Death (in a hospital).[127] See also: **negative patient care outcome.**

terminate with extreme prejudice. Assassinate; kill.[128] This term has become so well known, however, that it has lost its usefulness and is now seldom employed.

terminological inexactitude. Lie.[129]

terrain alteration. Saturation bombing.[130]

therapeutic misadventure. See: **diagnostic misadventure of high magnitude.**

therapeutic segregation. Solitary confinement.[131]

U **nclassified controlled information.** Government information that is not legally classifiable, but is withheld anyway. [132]

uncontained blade liberation. The breaking off of the blade of a helicopter rotor during flight—a term coined by the Federal Aviation Administration to explain a fatal helicopter crash.[133]

uncontained failure. A term used to describe what might have once been called an "explosion" in an engine of a United Air Lines plane in 1989. The plane crashed.[134]

using one's credibility for accomplishing an objective. An improvement upon "influence peddling," favored by former Secretary of the Interior James Watt.[135] Example: *Senator Alan Cranston* used *just about all of* **his credibility to accomplish the objective** *of shielding campaign contributor Charles Keating from federal bank regulators.*

Vvegetation manipulation. The Department of the Interior's term for the proposed clear-cutting of hundreds of acres of trees near Aspen, Colorado.[136]

very large, potentially disruptive reentry system. A nuclear-armed intercontinental ballistic missile, as described by U.S. Air Force Colonel Frank Horton.[137]

A **very large, potentially disruptive reentry system.**

visiting a site. A bombing attack. A second attack on the same target is called "revisiting a site."[138] See also: **service a target.**

Wwelcome. Warily acknowledge; grudgingly permit.[139] Example: *"We* **welcome** *comments from local residents."—The Nottingham (England) City Council.*

wildlife management. Killing, or permitting the hunting, of animals.[140] See also: **depopulation; harvesting.**

A **wildlife manager.**

BUREAUCRATICALLY UNSUITABLE/ BUREAUCRATICALLY SUITABLE

A person venturing into the world of the oppressor will find that a working knowledge of a *remarkably small* number of key words and phrases will give one virtually all the verbal tools necessary for success. Mastering the following short lexicon should give you all the vocabulary you'll need.

A

accident. Anomaly; event.

acid rain. Poorly buffered precipitation; atmospheric deposition of anthropogenically derived acidic substances.

antiabortion. Pro-life.

arms sales. Security assistance.

assassinate. See: kill.

B

bombing (the enemy). Air support; armed reconnaissance; servicing of a target; visitation of a site; terrain alteration.

bombing (one's own troops, presumably by mistake). Accidental delivery of ordnance equipment; friendly fire; incontinent ordnance.

D

dead. Nonviable; no longer a factor.

deforestation. Vegetation manipulation. See also: **murder** (of trees or animals).

depression. See: recession.

Fire (one employee). Dehire; decruit; deselect; indefinitely idle; involuntarily separate; nonrenew; outplace; present a career-change opportunity; redeploy; selectively separate; select out; vocationally relocate.

fire (many employees). Downsize; rightsize; streamline; degrow; destaff; rectify a work force imbalance; correct a redundancy of human resources; implement a skill-mix adjustment; manage down one's staff resources; engage in reduction activities.

Influence peddling. Using one's credibility for accomplishing an objective.

invasion. Preemptive counterattack.

Kill. Neutralize; alter the health of; render nonviable; arbitrarily deprive of life; terminate with extreme prejudice.

Lay off. See: fire.

lie. Categorical inaccuracy; counterfactual proposition; inoperative statement; strategic misrepresentation; terminological inexactitude.

loan, bad. Nonperforming asset.

lobbyist. Legislative leadership advocate.

lousy. Suboptimal.

M **murder (of people).** Arbitrary deprivation of life; executive action; health alteration; termination with extreme prejudice.

murder (of trees or animals). Depopulation; harvesting; management.

O **overthrow (a legitimate foreign government).** Destabilize.

P **police brutality.** Inappropriate physical abuse.

R **recession (or depression).** Meaningful downturn; period of economic adjustment; period of negative economic growth; temporary interruption of an economic expansion.

red tape. Procedural safeguards.

S **scab.** Noncertified worker.

sewage sludge. Organic biomass; regulated organic nutrients.

sneak attack (on a perceived enemy). Preemptive strike.

sneak attack (on oneself). Friendly fire; incontinent ordnance; accidental delivery of ordnance equipment.

stock market crash. Equity retreat.

T **tax increase.** Revenue enhancement; tax base broadening.
tax payments. Contributions; sacrifices.
torture. Aversion therapy.

U **"union-busting" legislation.** Right-to-work laws.

W **white collar crime.** Judgmental lapse; inappropriate behavior.
white only. Nonminority impacted.

SOURCE NOTES

PART I: A DICTIONARY OF POLITICALLY CORRECT (PC)
TERMS AND PHRASES

1. "Definitions," a handout authored by a Smith College administrator in collaboration with a group of student interns and published by the Smith College Office of Student Affairs in 1990. (The document, a "discussion paper" prepared as an orientation workshop project, does not, nor did it ever, represent the official policy of Smith College, which has somehow managed to survive into the 1990s without enacting a "language code" restricting student or faculty speech.)

2. Kramarae, Cheris and Treichler, Paula A., *A Feminist Dictionary,* Boston: Pandora Press, 1985, page 244.

3. Neaman, Judith S., and Silver, Carole G., *Kind Words,* New York: Avon Books, 1991, page 300.

4. D'Souza, Dinesh, *Illiberal Education: The Politics of Race and Sex on Campus,* New York: The Free Press, 1991, p. 98.

5. Marable, Manning, *How Capitalism Underdeveloped Black America,* Boston: South End Press, 1983, page 184.

6. Taylor, John, "Are You Politically Correct?" *New York,* January 21, 1991, page 39.

7. The American Hyphen Society.

8. Lutz, William, *Doublespeak,* New York: Harper Perennial, 1990, page 58.

9. Neaman, Judith S., and Silver, Carole G., *Kind Words,* New York: Avon Books, 1991, page 161.

10. Term coined by William Safire in his column "On Language," *The New York Times Magazine,* May 5, 1991, page 18.

11. "Definitions," handout published by the Smith College Office of Student Affairs, 1990.

12. Moore, Robert B., "Racist Stereotyping in the English Language," reprinted in Rothenberg, Paula S., *Racism and Sexism: An Integrated Study,* New York: St. Martin's Press, 1988, page 271.

13. *Dictionary of Cautionary Words and Phrases,* compiled by the Multicultural Management Fellows of the University of Missouri Journalism School.

14. Bell, Yvonne R., Bouie, Cathy L., and Baldwin, Joseph A., "Afrocentric Cultural Consciousness and African-American Male-Female Relationships," *Journal of Black Studies,* December 1990, pages 169–70.

15. Oyebade, Bayo, "African Studies and the Afrocentric Paradigm," *Journal of Black Studies,* December 1990, pages 234, 237.

16. "Definitions," handout published by the Smith College Office of Student Affairs, 1990.

17. Stewart, Ian, *The New Statesman*, October 22, 1987, cited in Rees, Nigel, *The Politically Correct Phrasebook*, London: Bloomsbury, 1993, page 11.

18. The Department of Rhetoric, University of California at Berkeley.

19. The American Hyphen Society.

20. The American Hyphen Society.

21. The American Hyphen Society.

22. Coined by linguist Suzette Haden Elgin, as cited in: Kramarae, Cheris, and Jenkins, Mercilee M., "Women Take Back the Talk," essay anthologized in: Penfield, Joyce, *Women and Language in Transition,* Albany: State University of New York Press, 1987, page 142.

23. Leo, John, "The new verbal order," *U.S. News & World Report,* July 22, 1991, page 14.

24. "Just Like Us?" *Harper's Magazine,* August 1988, page 50.

25. Scully, Vincent, remarks at a Yale University symposium on the humanities, cited in: Kimball, Roger, *Tenured Radicals,* New York: Harper Perennial, 1991, page 72.

26. Zak, Steven, "Ethics and Animals," *The Atlantic,* March 1989, page 70.

27. Earth First! founder Dave Foreman, paraphrased in *The Animals' Agenda,* July/August 1988, page 25.

28. Von Altendorf, Alan and Theresa, *Isms,* Memphis, TN: Mustang Publishing Company, 1991, page 8.

29. "Definitions," handout published by the Smith College Office of Student Affairs, 1990.

30. Cohen, Richard, "Academic Bondage," *The Washington Post Magazine,* May 5, 1991, page 11.

31. Lutz, William, "Doublespeak in Education," *Education Week,* November 29, 1989.

32. The Department of Rhetoric, University of California at Berkeley; Matthews, Anne, "Brave, New 'Cruelty Free' World," *The New York Times,* July 7, 1991.

33. Rees, Nigel, *The Politically Correct Phrasebook*, London: Bloomsbury, 1993, page 131.

34. Baron, Dennis, *Grammar and Gender,* New Haven, CT: Yale University Press, 1986, page 189.

35. *Newsweek,* February 5, 1990, page 20.

36. Sale, Kirkpatrick, *Dwellers in the Land: The Bioregional Vision,* San Francisco: Sierra Club Books, 1985; Foreman, Dave, *Confessions of an Eco-Warrior,* New York: Harmony Books, 1991.

37. Dumond, Val, *The Elements of Nonsexist Usage,* New York: Prentice Hall Press, 1990, page 82.

38. American Hyphen Society adoption consultant Skip Blumberg.

39. Glover, Diane, "The Need to Examine the Origin of Racism and Its Relationship to Skin-Color Devaluation," a "personal reflection" attached to *The Report of the Social Studies Syllabus Review and Development Committee* of the New York State Education Department, Albany: June 13, 1991, pages 77–79.

40. Clarke, Cheryl, "Lesbianism: An Act of Resistance," anthologized in *This Bridge Called My Back,* Latham, NY: Kitchen Table, Women of Color Press, 1983, page 128.

41. The American Hyphen Society.

42. Moran, Victoria, "Listening to Nature," *The Animals' Agenda,* July/August 1991, page 48.

43. Craig Lambert, associate editor, *Harvard Magazine,* interview with editors, December 2, 1991.

44. Taylor, John, "Are You Politically Correct?," *New York,* January 21, 1991, page 36.

45. Maryam Mohit, linguistics consultant to the American Hyphen Society.

46. The American Hyphen Society.

47. The American Hyphen Society.

48. Matthews, Anne, "Brave, New 'Cruelty Free' World," *The New York Times,* July 7, 1991.

49. *Dictionary of Cautionary Words and Phrases,* compiled by the 1989 Multicultural Management Program Fellows of the University of Missouri Journalism School.

50. Miller, Casey, and Swift, Kate, *The Handbook of Nonsexist Writing,* New York: Harper Perennial, 1988, page 33.

51. The American Hyphen Society.

52. The American Hyphen Society.

53. "Definitions," handout published by the Smith College Office of Student Affairs, 1990.

54. *The Quarterly Review of Doublespeak,* a publication of the National Council of Teachers of English, Urbana, Illinois, January 1991, page 2.

55. "Definitions," handout published by the Smith College Office of Student Affairs, 1990.

56. Rawson, Hugh, *A Dictionary of Euphemisms and Other Doubletalk,* New York: Crown Publishers, 1981, page 14.

57. *The New York Times,* March 12, 1993.

58. Rich, Adrienne, *On Lies, Secrets and Silence: Selected Prose 1966–1978,* New York: W. W. Norton, 1979, page 300.

59. The American Hyphen Society.

60. Walker, Alice, quoted in Kramarae, Cheris, and Treichler, Paula A., *A Feminist Dictionary,* Boston: Pandora Press, 1985, page 100.

61. Glover, Diane, "The Need to Examine the Origin of Racism and Its Relationship to Skin-Color Devaluation," a "personal reflection" attached to *The Report of the Social Studies Syllabus Review and Development Committee* of the New York State Education Department, Albany, June 13, 1991, pages 77–79.

62. Neaman, Judith S., and Silver, Carole G., *Kind Words,* New York: Avon Books, 1991, page 243.

63. Kramarae, Cheris, and Treichler, Paula A., *A Feminist Dictionary,* Boston: Pandora Press, 1985, pages 115–16.

64. "Words We Love to Hate," *The Disability Rag,* Winter 1990, page 15.

65. *The New York Times,* March 22, 1991, reprinted in *The Quarterly Review of Doublespeak,* a publication of the National Council of Teachers of English, Urbana, Illinois, April 1991, page 9.

66. Warland, Betsy, *Proper Deafinitions,* Vancouver: Press Gang Publishers, 1990, pages 61–62.

67. Pei, Mario, *Double-Speak in America,* Hawthorn Books, page 56.

68. Kramarae, Cheris, and Treichler, Paula A., *A Feminist Dictionary,* Boston: Pandora Press, 1985, page 99.

69. The American Hyphen Society.

70. Leo, John, "A political correctness roundup," *U.S. News & World Report,* June 22, 1992, page 29.

71. Castro, Janice, "Lost in Space: Common Sense," *Time,* July 6, 1992, page 13.

72. Leo, John, "A political correctness roundup," *U.S. News & World Report,* June 22, 1992, page 29.

73. Matthews, Anne, "Brave, New 'Cruelty Free' World," *The New York Times,* July 7, 1991.

74. Rees, Nigel, *The Politically Correct Phrasebook,* London: Bloomsbury, 1993, page 31.

75. Moore, Robert B., "Racist Stereotyping in the English Language," reprinted in Rothenberg, Paula S., *Racism and Sexism: An Integrated Study,* New York: St. Martin's Press, 1988, page 274.

76. Ball, Edward, "The White Issue," *The Village Voice,* May 18, 1993, page 27.

77. Rees, Nigel, *The Politically Correct Phrasebook,* London: Bloomsbury, 1993, page 31.

78. Koss, Mary P., "Changed Lives: The Psychological Impact of Sexual Harassment," anthologized in Paludi, Michele A., *Ivory Power: Sexual Harassment on Campus,* Albany: State University of New York Press, 1990, pages 74–75; Leo, John, "Don't oversimplify date rape," *U.S. News & World Report,* February 11, 1991, page 17; Rothbard, Murray N., "Date Rape," *National Review,* February 25, 1991, page 42.

79. Clarke, Cheryl, "Lesbianism: An Act of Resistance," anthologized in *This Bridge Called My Back,* Latham, NY, Kitchen Table, Women of Color Press, 1983, page 128.

80. Mayo, Anna, "A Coupla Decon Artists Sittin' Around Talkin'," *The Village Voice,* June 6, 1989, page 50.

81. Lutz, William, *Doublespeak,* New York: Harper Perennial, 1990, page 61.

82. The American Hyphen Society.

83. Matthews, Anne, "Brave, New 'Cruelty Free' World," *The New York Times,* July 7, 1991.

84. Asante, Molefi Kete, *Afrocentricity,* Trenton, NJ: Africa World Press, 1988, page 39.

85. Source for "dicktion": Warland, Betsy, *Proper Deafinitions,* Vancouver: Press Gang Publishers, 1990, page 21; source for "cuntionary": Kramarae, Cheris, and Treichler, Paula A., *A Feminist Dictionary,* Boston: Pandora Press, 1985, page 113.

86. Copeland, Gary A., "Face-ism and Primetime Television," *The Journal of Broadcasting and Electronic Media,* Spring 1989, pages 209–214.

87. "Definitions," handout published by the Smith College Office of Student Affairs, 1990.

88. The American Hyphen Society.

89. Castro, Janice, "Word Watch," *Time,* April 20, 1992, page 21.

90. The American Hyphen Society.

91. The American Hyphen Society.

92. The American Hyphen Society.

93. The American Hyphen Society.

94. Penelope, Julia, *Speaking Freely,* New York: Pergamon Press, 1990, page 209.

95. Leo, John, "The new verbal order," *U.S. News & World Report,* July 22, 1991, page 14.

96. Lutz, William, *Doublespeak,* New York: Harper Perennial, 1990, page 146.

97. Bishop, Katherine, "Stamping Out Perfume," *The New York Times,* September 12, 1991.

98. Leo, John, "The new verbal order," *U.S. News & World Report,* July 22, 1991, page 14.

99. Capek, Mary Ellen S., *A Woman's Thesaurus,* New York: Harper & Row, 1987, page 131.

100. D'Souza, Dinesh, *Illiberal Education,* New York: Free Press, 1991, page 214.

101. *The New York Times,* March 4, 1993, page A1.

102. Leo, John, "The new verbal order," *U.S. News & World Report,* July 22, 1991, page 14.

103. Hackney, Sheldon, "In the PC Wars, a Message from the Front," president's commencement address, University of Pennsylvania, May 21, 1991.

104. Source of term "ecofeminism": *The Animals' Agenda,* April 1990, page 15.

105. Source of quote: Morgan, Robin, "Q: Who *Can* We Trust? A: Ourselves," *Ms.,* September/October 1991, page 1.

106. Moore, Robert B., "Racist Stereotyping in the English Language," reprinted in Rothenberg, Paula S., *Racism and Sexism: An Integrated Study,* New York: St. Martin's Press, 1988, page 274.

107. *Christianity Today,* September 2, 1988, page 2, quoted in *The Quarterly Review of Doublespeak,* a publication of the National Council of Teachers of English, Urbana, Illinois, January, 1989, page 9.

108. LeMay, Harold, Lerner, Sid, and Taylor, Marian, *The New Words Dictionary,* New York: Ballantine Books, 1988, page 27.

109. Foreman, Dave, *Confessions of an Eco-Warrior,* New York: Harmony Books, 1991, page 124.

110. Goldfield, Bina, *The Efemcipated English Handbook,* New York: Westover Press, 1983, page 119.

111. Kramarae, Cheris, and Treichler, Paula A., *A Feminist Dictionary,* Boston: Pandora Press, 1985, pages 135–36.

112. Greenwald, John, "Word Watch," *Time,* December 21, 1992, page 15.

113. The American Hyphen Society.

114. Leeds Revolutionary Feminist Group, "Political Lesbianism: The Case Against Heterosexuality," 1981, quoted in Kramarae, Cheris, and Treichler, Paula A., *A Feminist Dictionary,* Boston: Pandora Press, 1985, page 137.

115. Baker, Robert, "'Pricks' and 'Chicks,'" reprinted in Rothenberg, Paula S., *Racism and Sexism: An Integrated Study,* New York: St. Martin's Press, 1988, page 274.

116. *The Report of the New York State Social Studies Review and Development Committee,* Albany, June 20, 1991, page 43.

117. Lutz, William, "Fourteen Years of Doublespeak," *College English,* March 1988, page 41.

118. Leo, John, "The political taboos of the '90s," *U.S. News & World Report,* March 4, 1991, page 21.

119. *Random House Webster's College Dictionary,* New York: Random House, 1991, page 449.

120. Daly, Mary, *Gyn/Ecology,* Boston: Beacon Press, 1978, page 8.

121. Dickson, Paul, *Slang!,* New York: Pocket Books, 1990, page 48.

122. "Definitions," handout published by the Smith College Office of Student Affairs, 1990.

123. Bell, Yvonne R., Bouie, Cathy L., and Baldwin, Joseph A., "Afrocentric Cultural Consciousness and African-American Male-Female Relationships," *Journal of Black Studies,* December 1990, pages 169–70.

124. Bell, Yvonne R., Bouie, Cathy L., and Baldwin, Joseph A., "Afrocentric Cultural Consciousness and African-American Male-Female Relationships," *Journal of Black Studies,* December 1990, pages 169–70.

125. Oyebade, Bayo, "African Studies and the Afrocentric Paradigm," *Journal of Black Studies,* December 1990, page 234.

126. Leo, John, "PC follies: The year in review," *U.S. News & World Report,* January 27, 1992, page 22.

127. Neaman, Judith S., and Silver, Carole G., *Kind Words,* New York: Avon Books, 1991, page 161.

128. Wright State University, Memorandum dated July 9, 1991, quoted in *The Quarterly Review of Doublespeak,* Urbana, Illinois, April 1992, page 3.

129. M. and J. Mohit, for the American Hyphen Society.

130. Copeland, Gary A., "Face-ism and Primetime Television," *The Journal of Broadcasting and Electronic Media,* Spring 1989, pages 209–14.

131. Taylor, John, "Are You Politically Correct?" *New York,* January 21, 1991, page 35.

132. Eichler, Margrit, *Nonsexist Research Methods,* Boston: Unwin Hyman, 1988, pages 114–15.

133. Levy, Jacob, "The Ennui of 'P.C.,'" *Brown Alumni Monthly,* October 1991, page 34.

134. *Sinister Wisdom* magazine, quoted in Kramarae, Cheris, and Treichler, Paula A., *A Feminist Dictionary,* Boston: Pandora Press, 1985, page 154.

135. Cooper, Tamsen, S., "A Pocket Perspective," *New Attitude,* quarterly newsletter of the National Association for the Advancement of Fat Acceptance Feminist Caucus, Northampton, MA, Fall 1991.

136. The American Hyphen Society.

137. The American Hyphen Society.

138. Goldfield, Bina, *The Efemcipated English Handbook,* New York: Westover Press, 1983, page 92.

139. Bright, Susie and Blank, Joani, editors, *Herotica 2: A Collection of Women's Erotic Fiction,* cited in *The Nation,* March 29, 1993, page 419.

140. Goldfield, Bina, *The Efemcipated English Handbook,* New York: Westover Press, 1983, page 94.

141. Goldfield, Bina, *The Efemcipated English Handbook,* New York: Westover Press, 1983, page 94.

142. Fausto-Sterling, Anne, "How Many Sexes Are There?", *The New York Times,* March 12, 1993, page A29.

143. Brenner, Marie, quoting her daughter Casey, in a *New York Times* op-ed piece, April 5, 1993.

144. McCarthy, Colman, "Euphemistic Language Makes the Gruesome Palatable," *The Washington Post,* 1990 column reprinted in *The Quarterly Review of Doublespeak,* a publication of the National Council of Teachers of English, Urbana, Illinois, July 1990, page 7.

145. The Department of Rhetoric, University of California at Berkeley.

146. "How to Speak Post-Modern, Being a Glossary of Actual Post-Modern Terminology in Current Usage Made Sensible for the Un/informed and Semi(initiated), Drawn from the book *Post-Modernism and the Social Sciences* by Pauline Marie Rosenau," pamphlet, Princeton, New Jersey: Princeton University Press, 1991.

147. The American Hyphen Society.

148. Leo, John, "The new verbal order," *U.S. News & World Report,* July 22, 1991, page 14.

149. Tsao, Emily, "How to Be Politically Incorrect," *Newsday,* September 1991.

150. Matthews, Anne, "Brave, New 'Cruelty Free' World," *The New York Times,* July 7, 1991.

151. Clinton, Kate, "Making Light," *Trivia: A Journal of Ideas,* Fall 1982, pages 38–39; quoted in Kramarae, Cheris, and Treichler, Paula A., *A Feminist Dictionary,* Boston: Pandora Press, 1985, page 171; Weisstein, Naomi, "Why We Aren't Laughing Anymore," *Ms.,* 1973 article, quoted in Penfield, Joyce, *Women and Language in Transition,* Albany: State University of New York Press, 1987, page 144.

152. Coward, Mat, "Backchat," *The New Statesman and Society,* May 31, 1991, page 47.

153. Fausto-Sterling, Anne, "How Many Sexes Are There?", *The New York Times,* March 12, 1993, page A29.

154. *Dictionary of Cautionary Words and Phrases,* compiled by the 1989 Multicultural Management Program Fellows of the University of Missouri Journalism School.

155. Miller, Casey and Swift, Kate, *The Handbook of Nonsexist Writing,* New York: Harper Perennial, 1988, page 134.

156. Frank, Francine Wattman, and Treichler, Paula A., *Language, Gender and Professional Writing,* New York: Modern Language Association, 1989, page 15.

157. Fury, Kathleen, "A Generous Fit," *New Woman,* February 1991, page 38.

158. The Department of Rhetoric, University of California at Berkeley, 1991 handout.

159. Goddard, Robert W., "Use Language Effectively," *Personnel Journal,* April 1989, page 32.

160. Macauley, Dave, "A New Paradigm," *The Animals' Agenda,* July/August 1988, page 50.

161. Lapham, Lewis H., "Acceptable Opinions," *Harper's Magazine,* December 1990.

162. Landers, Ann, syndicated column, October 20, 1988, cited in *The Quarterly Review of Doublespeak,* a publication of the National Council of Teachers of English, Urbana, Illinois, July 1989, page 10; Matthews, Anne, "Brave, New 'Cruelty Free' World," *The New York Times,* July 7, 1991.

163. Daly, Mary, *Gyn/Ecology,* Boston: Beacon Press, 1978, page xi.

164. Kramarae, Cheris, and Treichler, Paula A., *A Feminist Dictionary,* Boston: Pandora Press, 1985, page 184.

165. Castro, Janice, "Lost in Space: Common Sense," *Time,* July 6, 1992, page 13.

166. *Japan Economic Journal,* March 16, 1991, cited in *The Quarterly Review of Doublespeak,* a publication of the National Council of Teachers of English, Urbana, Illinois, April 1991, page 5.

167. The American Hyphen Society.

168. Matthews, Anne, "Brave, New 'Cruelty Free' World," *The New York Times,* July 7, 1991.

169. Stimpson, Catharine R., "On Differences," presidential address, Modern Language Association, New York City, 1990.

170. Von Altendorf, Alan and Theresa, *Isms,* Memphis, TN: Mustang Publishing Company, 1991, page 129.

171. Frank, Francine Wattman, and Treichler, Paula, *Language, Gender and Professional Writing: Theoretical Approaches and Guidelines for Nonsexist Usage,* New York: Modern Language Association, 1989, page 202.

172. Fausto-Sterling, Anne, "How Many Sexes Are There?", *The New York Times,* March 12, 1993, page A29.

173. *Random House Webster's College Dictionary,* New York: Random House, 1991, page 628.

174. Lennert, Midge, and Willson, Norma, *A Woman's New World Dictionary,* Lomita, CA: 51% Publications, 1973, pamphlet, quoted in Kramarae, Cheris, and Treichler, Paula A., *A Feminist Dictionary,* Boston: Pandora Press, 1985, page 190.

175. "Definitions," handout published by the Smith College Office of Student Affairs, 1990.

176. Clarke, Cheryl, "Lesbianism: An Act of Resistance," anthologized in *This Bridge Called My Back,* Latham, NY: Kitchen Table, Women of Color Press, 1983, pages 129–30.

177. Spender, Dr. Dale, *Man Made Language,* London: Pandora Press, 1990, page 177.

178. Frank, Francine Wattman, and Treichler, Paula A., *Language, Gender and Professional Writing: Theoretical Approaches and Guidelines for Nonsexist Usage,* New York: Modern Language Association, 1989, page 200.

179. Leo, John, "The new verbal order," *U.S. News & World Report,* July 22, 1991, page 14.

180. Leo, John, "The new verbal order," *U.S. News & World Report,* July 22, 1991, page 14.

181. "Definitions," handout published by the Smith College Office of Student Affairs, 1990.

182. Baron, Dennis, *Grammar and Gender,* New Haven: Yale University Press, 1986, pages 205–208.

183. Leo, John, "The political taboos of the '90s," *U.S. News & World Report,* March 4, 1991, page 21.

184. Goldfield, Bina, *The Efemcipated English Handbook,* New York: Westover Press, 1983, page 92.

185. Moran, Victoria, "Listening to Nature," *The Animals' Agenda,* July/August 1991, page 48.

186. *The Quarterly Review of Doublespeak,* Urbana, Illinois, October 1992, page 8.

187. Goodman, Susan, *The Philadelphia Inquirer,* October 19, 1992. Reprinted in *The Quarterly Review of Doublespeak,* Urbana, Illinois, July 1992, page 15.

188. *The Quarterly Review of Doublespeak,* a publication of the National Council of Teachers of English, Urbana, Illlinois, April 1991, page 3.

189. Safire, William, *Language Maven Strikes Again,* New York: Henry Holt and Company, 1991, page 368.

190. Castro, Janice, "Word Watch," *Time,* April 20, 1992, page 21.

191. Decker, Timothy, "Pressure to Conform," *The Vassar Spectator,* March/April 1991, page 7.

192. Mayo, Anna, "A Coupla Decon Artists Sittin' Around Talkin'," *The Village Voice,* June 6, 1989, page 50.

193. The American Hyphen Society.

194. Kramarae, Cheris, and Treichler, Paula A., *A Feminist Dictionary,* Boston: Pandora Press, 1985, page 203.

195. Mooney, Carolyn J., "N.Y. City College Panel to Weigh Academic Freedom, Inflammatory Racial Views of 2 Faculty Members," *The Chronicle of Higher Education,* May 23, 1990, pages A13, A17.

196. U.S. Department of Labor, *Job Title Revisions to Eliminate Sex- and Age-Referent Language from the Dictionary of Occupational Titles,* Washington, D.C., 1975, page 59.

197. The American Hyphen Society.

198. "Definitions," handout published by the Smith College Office of Student Affairs, 1990.

199. "Definitions," handout published by the Smith College Office of Student Affairs, 1990.

200. Three Rivers, Amoja, *Cultural Etiquette: A Guide for the Well-Intentioned,* Indian Valley, Virginia: Market Wimmin, 1990, page 10.

201. Lutz, William, *Doublespeak,* New York: Harper Perennial, 1990, page 133.

202. Allen, Pamela Payne, "Taking the Next Step in Inclusive Language," *The Christian Century,* April 23, 1986, page 410.

203. Lutz, William, "Fourteen Years of Doublespeak," *English Journal,* March 1988, page 42.

204. Matthews, Anne, "Brave, New 'Cruelty Free' World," *The New York Times,* July 7, 1991.

205. Leo, John, "Reading between the hyphens," *U.S. News & World Report,* May 21, 1990, page 23.

206. *Executive Recruiter News,* Fitzwilliam, New Hampshire, November 1990.

207. Streitfeld, David, "Terms of Abuse," *The Washington Post,* July 2, 1991, page E5; Leo, John, "The new verbal order," *U.S. News & World Report,* July 22, 1991, page 14.

208. Snyder, Dia, American Hyphen Society social relations consultant.

209. "Definitions," handout published by the Smith College Office of Student Affairs, 1990.

210. Frank, Francine Wattman, and Treichler, Paula, *Language, Gender and Professional Writing: Theoretical Approaches and Guidelines for Nonsexist Usage,* New York: Modern Language Association, 1989, page 231.

211. Three Rivers, Amoja, *Cultural Etiquette: A Guide for the Well-Intentioned,* Indian Valley, Virginia: Market Wimmin, 1990, page 11.

212. Fausto-Sterling, Anne, "How Many Sexes Are There?", *The New York Times,* March 12, 1993, page A29.

213. Cited by American Hyphen Society field representative Arlene Sherman.

214. Blumberg, Skip, American Hyphen Society; also *Random House Webster's College Dictionary,* New York: Random House, 1991, page 709.

215. Yamada, Mitsuye, "Invisibility is an Unnatural Disaster," reprinted in Moraga, Cherrié, and Anzaldúa, Gloria, eds., *This Bridge Called My Back: Writings by Radical Women of Color,* New York: Kitchen Table: Women of Color Press, 1983, page 35.

216. Lutz, William, *Doublespeak,* New York: Harper Perennial, 1990, page 133.

217. The American Hyphen Society.

218. Raimi, Jessica, "By Any Other Name," *Columbia,* Spring 1991, page 36.

219. *Dictionary of Cautionary Words and Phrases,* compiled by the 1989 Multicultural Management Fellows of the University of Missouri Journalism School.

220. Asante, Molefi Kete, *Afrocentricity,* Trenton, NJ: Africa World Press, 1988, page 41.

221. Withan, Geoffrey, *The Vassar Spectator,* March/April 1991.

222. Lutz, William, *Doublespeak,* New York: Harper Perennial, 1990, page 63.

223. *Random House Webster's College Dictionary,* New York: Random House, 1991, page 754; Rees, Nigel, *The Politically Correct Phrasebook,* London: Bloomsbury, 1993, page 84; and the *Grolier On-Line Encyclopedia,* accessed through AppleLink, June 21, 1993.

224. Matthews, Anne, "Brave, New 'Cruelty Free' World," *The New York Times,* July 7, 1991.

225. Anthologized in Hageman, Alice, *Sexist Religion and Women in the Church: No More Silence!* New York: Association Press, pages 125–42.

226. Membership advertisement, *New Attitude,* publication of the Feminist Caucus of the National Association for the Advancement of Fat Acceptance, Fall 1991, page 9.

227. "Definitions," handout published by the Smith College Office of Student Affairs, 1990.

228. Gonzales, David, "What's the Problem with 'Hispanic'? Just Ask a 'Latino'," *The New York Times*, November 15, 1992, Section 4, page E6.

229. Lutz, William, *Doublespeak*, New York: Harper Perennial, 1990, page 106.

230. Davenport, Doris, quoted in Kramarae, Cheris, and Treichler, Paula A., *A Feminist Dictionary*, Boston: Pandora Press, 1985, page 230.

231. Mitchell, Felicia, "Including Women at Emory & Henry College: Evolution of an Inclusive Language Policy," *Women's Studies Quarterly*, Spring 1990, page 223.

232. Lentricchia, Frank, and McLaughlin, Thomas, *Critical Terms for Literary Study*, Chicago: University of Chicago Press, 1991, page 1.

233. D'Souza, Dinesh, *Illiberal Education*, New York: Free Press, 1991, page 180.

234. Taylor, John, "Are You Politically Correct?," *New York*, January 21, 1991, page 36.

235. "How to Speak Post-Modern, Being a Glossary of Actual Post-Modern Terminology in Current Usage Made Sensible for the Un/informed and Semi(initiated), Drawn from the book *Post-Modernism and the Social Sciences* by Pauline Marie Rosenau," pamphlet, Princeton, New Jersey: Princeton University Press, 1991.

236. Rawson, Hugh, *A Dictionary of Euphemisms and Other Doubletalk*, New York: Crown Publishers, 1981, page 249.

237. "Definitions," handout published by the Smith College Office of Student Affairs, 1990.

238. Dumond, Val, *The Elements of Nonsexist Usage: A Guide to Inclusive Spoken and Written English*, Prentice Hall, 1990, page 82.

239. Daly, Mary, *Websters' First New Intergalactic Wickedary of the English Language*, Boston: Beacon Press, 1987, page 210.

240. Kramarae, Cheris, and Treichler, Paula A., *A Feminist Dictionary*, Boston: Pandora Press, 1985, page 244. Attributed to Mary Daly; italics appear in the original quotation.

241. Kramarae, Cheris, and Treichler, Paula A., *A Feminist Dictionary*, Boston: Pandora Press, 1985, page 245.

242. Rifkin, Mark E., Letter to *The Animals' Agenda*, July/August 1991, page 8.

243. Kramarae, Cheris, and Treichler, Paula A., *A Feminist Dictionary*, Boston: Pandora Press, 1985, page 244.

244. *Random House Webster's College Dictionary*, New York: Random House, 1991, page 829.

245. The American Hyphen Society.

246. The Department of Rhetoric, University of California at Berkeley, 1991 handout.

247. *Campus Report*, June 1988, pages 1, 8. As cited in D'Souza, Dinesh, *Illiberal Education*, New York: Free Press, 1991, page 259.

248. The New Jersey State Crime Control Commission, quoted in Lutz, William, "Fourteen Years of Doublespeak," *English Journal,* March 1988, page 41.

249. Glover, Diane, "The Need to Examine the Origin of Racism and Its Relationship to Skin-Color Devaluation," a "personal reflection" attached to *The Report of the Social Studies Syllabus Review and Development Committee* of the New York State Education Department, Albany, June 13, 1991, pages 77–79.

250. Welsing, Frances, "The Cress Theory of Color Confrontation and Racism," quoted in Kunjufu, Jawanza, *Countering the Conspiracy to Destroy Black Boys,* Chicago: African American Images, 1985, page 2.

251. *The Philadelphia Inquirer,* March 6, 1992, page D1. Quoted in *The Quarterly Review of Doublespeak,* Urbana, Illinois, October 1992, page 8.

252. Streitfeld, David, "Terms of Abuse," *The Washington Post,* July 2, 1991, page E5.

253. Fausto-Sterling, Anne, "How Many Sexes Are There?", *The New York Times,* March 12, 1993, page A29.

254. The Department of Rhetoric, University of California at Berkeley, 1991 handout.

255. The Mineral Rights Task Force of the American Hyphen Society.

256. *Random House Webster's College Dictionary,* New York: Random House, 1991, page 866.

257. Asante, Molefi Kete, "Putting Africa at the Center," *Newsweek,* September 23, 1991, page 46.

258. Daly, Mary, *Gyn/Ecology,* Boston: Beacon Press, 1978, page 239.

259. Leo, John, "The new verbal order," *U.S. News & World Report,* July 22, 1991, page 14.

260. The American Hyphen Society.

261. Dickson, Paul, *Slang!,* New York: Pocket Books, 1990, page 50.

262. The American Hyphen Society.

263. Based on a report by Janice Castro in *Time,* April 20, 1992, page 21.

264. Gates, Henry Louis, Jr., "Multicultist," *The Voice Literary Supplement,* October 1991, pages 18–19.

265. Jones, Lisa, "How I Invented Multiculturalism," *The Village Voice,* December 3, 1991, page 51.

266. Executive Summary of *The Report of the New York State Social Studies Review and Development Committee,* Albany, June 20, 1991.

267. Welsing, Frances, "The Cress Theory of Color Confrontation and Racism," quoted in Kunjufu, Jawanza, *Countering the Conspiracy to Destroy Black Boys,* Chicago: African American Images, 1985, page 2.

268. Frank, Francine Wattman, and Treichler, Paula A., *Language, Gender and Professional Writing: Theoretical Approaches and Guidelines for Nonsexist Usage,* New York: Modern Language Association, 1989, page 19.

269. Blumberg, Skip, Native Alaskan consultant, American Hyphen Society.

270. Lutz, William, *Doublespeak,* New York: Harper Perennial, 1990, page 61.

271. Smith, Jack, "Clearly, It's a Plastic Language With Devious Overtones," *Los Angeles Times,* October 24, 1990, page E6.

272. Neaman, Judith S., and Silver, Carole G., *Kind Words,* New York: Avon Books, 1991, page 323.

273. Maryam Mohit, American Hyphen Society linguistics consultant.

274. The American Hyphen Society.

275. The American Hyphen Society.

276. Lutz, William, *Doublespeak*, New York: Harper Perennial, 1990, page 1.

277. Singer, Peter, *In Defense of Animals,* New York: Harper Perennial, 1986, page 210.

278. Leo, John, "The political taboos of the '90s," *U.S. News & World Report,* March 4, 1991, page 21.

279. London: *The Sunday Times,* March 22, 1992, quoted in Rees, Nigel, *The Politically Correct Phrasebook,* London: Bloomsbury, 1993, page 5.

280. *New England Journal of Medicine,* August 18, 1988. Cited in *The Quarterly Review of Doublespeak,* a publication of the National Council of Teachers of English, Urbana, Illinois, January 1989, page 9.

281. "Definitions," handout published by the Smith College Office of Student Affairs, 1990.

282. The American Hyphen Society.

283. The American Hyphen Society.

284. Leo, John, "The political taboos of the '90s," *U.S. News & World Report,* March 4, 1991, page 21.

285. Clifton, Merritt, "Animal Newsline," *The Animals' Agenda,* May 1991, page 37.

286. Streitfeld, David, "Terms of Abuse," *The Washington Post,* July 2, 1991, page E5.

287. The American Hyphen Society.

288. Jones, Lisa, "Open Letter to a Brother," *The Village Voice,* October 8, 1991, page 45.

289. Lorde, Audre, "Age, Race, Class and Sex: Women Redefining Difference," a paper delivered at the Copeland Colloquium, Amherst College, April 1980, and reprinted in Rothenberg, Paula S., *Racism and Sexism: An Integrated Study,* New York: St. Martin's Press, 1988, page 352.

290. "Definitions," handout published by the Smith College Office of Student Affairs, 1990.

291. Trudeau, Garry, address at Yale University's Class Day, May, 1991, excerpted in *Harper's Magazine,* October 1991, page 40.

292. The American Hyphen Society.

293. Leo, John, "The new verbal order," *U.S. News & World Report,* July 22, 1991, page 14.

294. Dunayer, Eric, "Caring for Other Animals," regular column in *The Animals' Agenda*.

295. Kramarae, Cheris, and Treichler, Paula A., *A Feminist Dictionary*, Boston: Pandora Press, 1985, page 317.

296. Frank, Francine Wattman, and Treichler, Paula A., *Language, Gender and Professional Writing: Theoretical Approaches and Guidelines for Nonsexist Usage*, New York: Modern Language Association, 1989, page 201.

297. Cited by American Hyphen Society consultant Juliet Mohit.

298. Maryam Mohit, American Hyphen Society.

299. Moore, Robert B., "Racist Stereotyping in the English Language," reprinted in Rothenberg, Paula S., *Racism and Sexism: An Integrated Study*, New York: St. Martin's Press, 1988, page 274.

300. Unnamed professor at Washington University, St. Louis, cited by Christina Hoff Summers of the Clark University Department of Philosophy in an unpublished manuscript, quoted in D'Souza, Dinesh, *Illiberal Education*, Free Press, 1991.

301. Frank, Francine Wattman, and Treichler, Paula A., *Language, Gender and Professional Writing: Theoretical Approaches and Guidelines for Nonsexist Usage*, New York: Modern Language Association, 1989, page 199.

302. Foreman, Dave, *Confessions of an Eco-Warrior*, New York: Harmony Books, 1991, page 45.

303. The Department of Rhetoric, University of California at Berkeley, 1991 handout.

304. Amiel, Barbara, "The Frightening Tyranny of Language," *Maclean's Magazine*, December 31, 1990, page 9.

305. Phillips, Lisa, "No Man's Land: At the Threshold of a Millennium," *1993 Biennial Exhibition*, catalog, New York: Whitney Museum of American Art in Association with Harry N. Abrams, Inc., 1993, pages 53-55.

306. Daly, Mary, *Gyn/Ecology*, Beacon Press: 1978, page 1.

307. The American Hyphen Society.

308. Taylor, John, "Are You Politically Correct?" *New York*, January 21, 1991, page 37.

309. "Contest Results in New Phrase Designed to Focus on the Abilities of People with Disabilities," press release distributed by the National Cristina Foundation, Pelham Manor, NY, March 5, 1991.

310. Rawson, Hugh, *A Dictionary of Euphemisms and Other Doubletalk*, New York: Crown Publishers, 1981, page 210.

311. Allan, Keith, and Burridge, Kate, *Euphemism and Dysphemism*, New York: Oxford University Press, 1991, page 190.

312. Neaman, Judith S., and Silver, Carole G., *Kind Words*, New York: Avon Books, 1991, page 305.

313. Lorde, Audre, "Age, Race, Class and Sex: Women Redefining Difference," a paper delivered at the Copeland Colloquium, Amherst College, April 1980, and reprinted in Rothenberg, Paula S., *Racism and Sexism: An Integrated*

Study, New York: St. Martin's Press, 1988, page 355. Lorde prefers to spell "Color," used in this context, with a capital "C"; "people of color" with a lower-case "c" is perhaps more common.

314. Source of Matthews quote: Matthews, Anne, "Brave, New 'Cruelty Free' World," *The New York Times,* July 7, 1991.

315. Kramarae, Cheris, and Treichler, Paula A., *A Feminist Dictionary,* Boston: Pandora Press, 1985, page 499.

316. The American Hyphen Society.

317. Donne, Faith, professor of education at Dartmouth College. Cited by Craig Lambert, *Harvard Magazine,* in an interview with the authors, December 2, 1991.

318. Kramarae, Cheris, and Treichler, Paula A., *A Feminist Dictionary,* Boston: Pandora Press, 1985, page 52.

319. The National Association to Advance Fat Acceptance, Feminist Caucus, whose slogan is "Women of Substance/Women of Power."

320. Sorrels, Bobbye D., *The Nonsexist Communicator: Solving the Problems of Gender and Awkwardness in the English Language,* Englewood Cliffs, NJ: Prentice Hall, 1983; cited in Baron, Dennis, *Grammar and Gender,* New Haven, CT: Yale University Press, 1986, page 189.

321. Lutz, William, *Doublespeak,* New York: Harper Perennial, 1989, page 227.

322. Taylor, John, "Are You Politically Correct?," *New York,* January 21, 1991, page 38.

323. Source of term: Françoise Parturier, quoted in Partnow, Elaine, *The Quotable Woman,* Los Angeles: Pinnacle Books, 1977; source of Rich quotation: Rich, B Ruby, "Top Girl: The Paglia Paradox," *The Village Voice,* October 8, 1991, page 29.

324. Daly, Mary, *Websters' First New Intergalactic Wickedary of the English Language,* Boston: Beacon Press, 1987, page 216.

325. Leo, John, "A political correctness roundup," *U.S. News & World Report,* June 22, 1992, page 29.

326. Lutz, William, *Doublespeak,* New York: Harper Perennial, 1990, page 64.

327. The American Hyphen Society.

328. Leo, John, "A political correctness roundup," *U.S. News & World Report,* June 22, 1992, page 31.

329. The American Hyphen Society.

330. Matthews, Anne, "Brave, New 'Cruelty Free' World," *The New York Times,* July 7, 1991.

331. Blumberg, Lisa, letter published in *The Disability Rag,* Winter 1990, page 2.

332. Allan, Keith, and Burridge, Kate, *Euphemism and Dysphemism,* New York: Oxford University Press, 1991, page 190.

333. *Random House Webster's College Dictionary,* New York: Random House, 1991, page 1040.

334. Pei, Mario, *Double-Speak in America,* New York: Hawthorn Books, 1973, page 55.

335. "Gala Pomo Issue," *The Village Voice Literary Supplement,* October 1991.

336. Rosenau, Pauline Marie, *Post-Modernism and the Social Sciences,* Princeton, NJ: Princeton University Press, 1992.

337. Safire, William, *Language Maven Strikes Again,* New York: Henry Holt and Company, 1991; Three Rivers, Amoja, *Cultural Etiquette: A Guide for the Well-Intentioned,* Indian Valley, Virginia: Market Wimmin, 1990, page 5.

338. The American Hyphen Society.

339. Sheshol, Jeff, "Politically Correct Person," comic strip, reprinted in *Newsweek,* December 24, 1990, page 53.

340. Lapham, Lewis H., "Acceptable Opinions," *Harper's Magazine,* December 1990.

341. "How to Speak Post-Modern, Being a Glossary of Actual Post-Modern Terminology in Current Usage Made Sensible for the Un/informed and Semi(initiated), Drawn from the book *Post-Modernism and the Social Sciences* by Pauline Marie Rosenau," pamphlet, Princeton, New Jersey: Princeton University Press, 1991.

342. The Department of Rhetoric, University of California at Berkeley, handout, 1991; McCarthy, Colman, "Euphemistic Language Makes the Gruesome Palatable," *Washington Post* column reprinted in *The Quarterly Review of Doublespeak,* a publication of the National Council of Teachers of English, Urbana, Illinois, July 1990, page 7.

343. The Department of Rhetoric, University of California at Berkeley, 1991 handout.

344. Leo, John, "The new verbal order," *U.S. News & World Report,* July 22, 1991, page 14.

345. Allan, Keith, and Burridge, Kate, *Euphemism and Dysphemism,* New York: Oxford University Press, 1991, page 190.

346. "Definitions," handout published by the Smith College Office of Student Affairs, 1990.

347. Leo, John, "The new verbal order," *U.S. News & World Report,* July 22, 1991, page 14.

348. Zalk, Sue Rosenberg, "Men in the Academy," anthologized in Paludi, Michele A., *Ivory Power: Sexual Harassment on Campus,* Albany: State University of New York Press, 1990, page 153.

349. Kaye, Melanie, "Some Notes on Jewish Lesbian Identity," anthologized in Beck, Evelyn Torton, *Nice Jewish Girls,* Watertown, MA: Persephone, 1982, page 38.

350. Lipton, James, "Left Out," *The New York Times Magazine,* September 8, 1991.

351. Lapham, Lewis H., "Acceptable Opinions," *Harper's Magazine,* December 1990.

352. Leo, John, "The lingo of entitlement," *U.S. News & World Report*, October 14, 1991, page 22.

353. Leo, John, "The lingo of entitlement," *U.S. News & World Report*, October 14, 1991, page 22.

354. Maurer, Marc, "Language and the Future of the Blind [sic]," speech delivered at the banquet of the Annual Convention of the National Federation of the Blind, July 8, 1989, reprinted in *Vital Speeches of the Day.*

355. Leo, John, "The political taboos of the '90s," *U.S. News & World Report*, March 4, 1991, page 21.

356. McCarthy, Colman, "Euphemistic Language Makes the Gruesome Palatable," 1990 column in *The Washington Post*, reprinted in *The Quarterly Review of Doublespeak*, a publication of the National Council of Teachers of English, Urbana, Illinois, July 1990, page 7.

357. The American Hyphen Society.

358. Neaman, Judith S., and Silver, Carole G., *Kind Words*, New York: Avon Books, 1991, page 300.

359. Neaman, Judith S., and Silver, Carole G., *Kind Words*, New York: Avon Books, 1991, page 166.

360. The American Hyphen Society.

361. Neaman, Judith S., and Silver, Carole G., *Kind Words*, New York: Avon Books, 1991, page 166.

362. Frye, Marilyn, *The Politics of Reality: Essays in Feminist Theory*, Trumansburg, NY: The Crossing Press, 1983, page 104; quoted in Kramarae, Cheris, and Treichler, Paula A., *A Feminist Dictionary*, Boston: Pandora Press, 1985, page 407.

363. *The Disability Rag*, Winter 1990, page 14.

364. Dumond, Val, *The Elements of Nonsexist Usage*, New York: Prentice Hall Press, 1990, page 85.

365. *The Quarterly Review of Doublespeak*, a publication of the National Council of Teachers of English, Urbana, Illlinois, October, 1991, page 4.

366. "Definitions," handout published by the Smith College Office of Student Affairs, 1990.

367. Lutz, William, *Doublespeak*, New York: Harper Perennial, 1990, page 67.

368. Gusewelle, C. W., "Perils Still Abound—Only Their Names Are Gentler," article in *The Kansas City Star*, reprinted in *The Quarterly Review of Doublespeak*, a publication of the National Council of Teachers of English, Urbana, Illlinois, July 1990, page 8.

369. *The Toronto Sun*, September 6, 1991, quoted in *The Quarterly Review of Doublespeak*, Urbana, Illinois, April 1992, page 9.

370. Taylor, John, "Men on Trial," *New York*, December 16, 1991, page 34.

371. McClintock, Anne, "Safe Sluts," *The Village Voice*, August 20, 1991, page 26.

372. Spender, Dale, *Women of Ideas and What Men Have Done to Them*, London:

Routledge and Kegan Paul, 1982, page 341, quoted in Kramarae, Cheris, and Treichler, Paula A., *A Feminist Dictionary*, Boston: Pandora Press, 1985, page 362.

373. Angelou, Maya, quoted in Frank, Francine Wattman, and Treichler, Paula A., *Language, Gender and Professional Writing: Theoretical Approaches and Guidelines for Nonsexist Usage*, New York: Modern Language Association, 1989, pages 200, 202.

374. Safire, William, "Meet My Whatsit," *The New York Times Magazine*, November 9, 1986, page 10.

375. The American Hyphen Society.

376. Lipton, James, "Left Out," *The New York Times Magazine*, September 8, 1991.

377. Hemenway, Carrie, "From the Coordinator," *New Attitude*, publication of the Feminist Caucus of the National Association for the Advancement of Fat Acceptance, Fall 1991, page 2.

378. Kramarae, Cheris, and Treichler, Paula A., *A Feminist Dictionary*, Boston: Pandora Press, 1985, page 154.

379. Welsing, Frances, "The Cress Theory of Color Confrontation and Racism," quoted in Kunjufu, Jawanza, *Countering the Conspiracy to Destroy Black Boys*, Chicago: African American Images, 1985, page 2.

380. Kunjufu, Jawanza, *Countering the Conspiracy to Destroy Black Boys*, Chicago: African American Images, 1985, page 2.

381. Welsing, Frances, "The Cress Theory of Color Confrontation and Racism," quoted in Kunjufu, Jawanza, *Countering the Conspiracy to Destroy Black Boys*, Chicago: African American Images, 1985, page 2.

382. Dumond, Val, *The Elements of Nonsexist Usage*, New York: Prentice Hall, 1990, page 86.

383. The American Hyphen Society.

384. The Department of Rhetoric, University of California at Berkeley, 1991 handout.

385. The American Hyphen Society.

386. Neaman, Judith S., and Silver, Carole G., *Kind Words*, New York: Avon Books, 1991, page 161.

387. The American Hyphen Society.

388. Singer, Peter, *Animal Liberation*, New York: Avon Books, 1990, page 243; Withan, Geoffrey, "Politically Incorrect and Proud of It," *The Vassar Spectator*, March/April 1991, page 22.

389. Barnard, Neal D., M.D., "The Psychology of Abuse," *The Animals' Agenda*, June 1991, page 51.

390. Kramarae, Cheris, and Jenkins, Mercilee M., "Women Take Back the Talk," anthologized in *Women and Language in Transition*, edited by Joyce Penfield, Albany: State University of New York Press, 1987, page 141.

391. *The San Diego Union-Tribune,* August 2, 1992, cited in *The Quarterly Review of Doublespeak,* Urbana, Illinois, April 1993, page 5.

392. The American Hyphen Society.

393. Neuschel, Kristin, Professor of History, Department of Women's Studies, Duke University, quoted by her former student Karen Larsen Meizels, of the American Hyphen Society.

394. Sager, Mike, "Inhuman Bondage," *Rolling Stone,* March 24, 1988, page 90.

395. Miller, Casey, and Swift, Kate, *The Handbook of Nonsexist Writing,* New York: Harper, 1988, page 161.

396. Capek, Mary Ellen S., *A Woman's Thesaurus,* New York: Harper & Row, 1987, page 201.

397. Pei, Mario, *Double-Speak in America,* New York: Hawthorn Books, 1973, page 67.

398. Leo, John, "The new verbal order," *U.S. News & World Report,* July 22, 1991, page 14.

399. Dickson, Paul, *Slang!,* New York: Pocket Books, 1990, page 52.

400. The American Hyphen Society.

401. Phillips, Lisa, "No Man's Land: At the Threshold of a Millennium," *1993 Biennial Exhibition,* catalog, New York: Whitney Museum of American Art in Association with Harry N. Abrams, Inc., 1993, pages 53-54.

402. Mooney, Carolyn J., "N.Y. City College Panel to Weigh Academic Freedom, Inflammatory Racial Views of 2 Faculty Members," *The Chronicle of Higher Education,* May 23, 1990, pages A13, A17.

403. Leo, John, "The new verbal order," *U.S. News & World Report,* July 22, 1991, page 14.

404. Leo, John, "A political correctness roundup," *U.S. News & World Report,* June 22, 1992, page 29.

405. Kramarae, Cheris, and Treichler, Paula A., *A Feminist Dictionary,* Boston: Pandora Press, 1985, pages 444-45.

406. Abernathy, Joe, "Sex and the Single Hacker," *The Village Voice,* March 16, 1993, page 49.

407. The American Hyphen Society.

408. "Definitions," handout published by the Smith College Office of Student Affairs, 1990.

409. Osman, Sonia, "A to Z of Feminism," *Spare Rib,* November 27–30, 1983, page 29. Quoted in: Kramarae, Cheris, and Treichler, Paula A., *A Feminist Dictionary,* Boston: Pandora Press, 1985, pages 444-45.

410. The Department of Rhetoric, University of California at Berkeley.

411. *The Chicago Tribune,* August 27, 1991, "Tempo" section, page 1. As cited in *The Quarterly Review of Doublespeak,* a publication of the National Council of Teachers of English, Urbana, Illinois, January 1990, page 7.

412. The American Hyphen Society.

413. The American Hyphen Society.

414. Attributed to Alan Alda. Source: Kramarae, Cheris, and Treichler, Paula A., *A Feminist Dictionary,* Boston: Pandora Press, 1985, pages 455–56.

415. "How to Speak Post-Modern, Being a Glossary of Actual Post-Modern Terminology in Current Usage Made Sensible for the Un/informed and Semi(initiated), Drawn from the Book *Post-Modernism and the Social Sciences* by Pauline Marie Rosenau," pamphlet, Princeton, New Jersey: Princeton University Press, 1991.

416. Rich, B Ruby, "Top Girl," *The Village Voice,* October 8, 1991, page 33.

417. Miller, Casey, and Swift, Kate, "What About New Human Pronouns?", *Current* magazine, Number 138, pages 43–48, quoted in Baron, Dennis, *Grammar and Gender,* New Haven: Yale University Press, 1986, pages 206, 212.

418. The American Hyphen Society.

419. Bernstein, Richard, "When Parentheses Are Transgressive," *The New York Times,* 1990, reprinted in *The Quarterly Review of Doublespeak,* a publication of the National Council of Teachers of English, Urbana, Illinois, October 1991, page 11.

420. Cited in Foreman, Dave, *Confessions of an Eco-Warrior,* New York: Harmony Books, 1991, page 45; also cited in Jack, Alex, *The New Age Dictionary,* Brookline, MA: Kanthaka Press, 1976, page 205.

421. Fausto-Sterling, Anne, "How Many Sexes Are There?", *The New York Times,* March 12, 1993, page A29.

422. *The Quarterly Review of Doublespeak,* a publication of the National Council of Teachers of English, Urbana, Illlinois, April 1991, pages 8–9.

423. Leo, John, "The new verbal order," *U.S. News & World Report,* July 22, 1991, page 14.

424. Leo, John, "The new verbal order," *U.S. News & World Report,* July 22, 1991, page 14.

425. The American Hyphen Society.

426. The American Hyphen Society.

427. Based on views expressed by Dr. Dale Spender in *Women of Ideas and What Men Have Done to Them,* London: Routledge and Kegan Paul, 1982, page 341, quoted in Kramarae, Cheris, and Treichler, Paula A., *A Feminist Dictionary,* Boston: Pandora Press, 1985, page 362.

428. The American Hyphen Society.

429. *Ms.,* July/August 1991, page 15.

430. The Department of Rhetoric, University of California at Berkeley, 1991 handout.

431. Dumond, Val, *The Elements of Nonsexist Usage: A Guide to Inclusive Spoken and Written English,* Prentice Hall, 1990, page 82.

432. Spender, Dr. Dale, *Man Made Language,* London: Pandora Press, 1990, page 182.

433. Baron, Dennis, *Grammar and Gender,* New Haven: Yale University Press, 1986, page 206.

434. Matthews, Anne, "Brave, New 'Cruelty Free' World," *The New York Times*, July 7, 1991.

435. Lutz, William, "Fourteen Years of Doublespeak," *College English*, March 1988, page 41.

436. Taylor, John, "Are You Politically Correct?," *New York*, January 21, 1991, page 37.

437. Trudeau, Garry, address at Yale University's Class Day, May 1991, excerpted in *Harper's Magazine*, October 1991, page 40.

438. The Department of Rhetoric, University of California at Berkeley, 1991 handout.

439. The American Hyphen Society.

440. *The Animals' Voice*, advertisement in *The Animals' Agenda*, July/August 1988, inside back cover.

441. Foreman, Dave, *Confessions of an Eco-Warrior*, New York: Harmony Books, 1991, page 49.

442. Rees, Nigel, *The Politically Correct Phrasebook*, London: Bloomsbury, 1993, page 131.

443. *Random House Webster's College Dictionary*, New York: Random House, 1991.

444. Von Altendorf, Alan and Theresa, *Isms*, Memphis, TN: Mustang Publishing Company, 1991, page 325.

445. Berman, Paul, *Debating P.C.*, New York: Laurel, 1992, Introduction, page 14.

446. The Department of Rhetoric, University of California at Berkeley, 1991 handout.

447. Source of Lorde quotes: Lorde, Audre, "Age, Race, Class and Sex: Women Redefining Difference," a paper delivered at the Copeland Colloquium, Amherst College, April 1980, and reprinted in Rothenberg, Paula S., *Racism and Sexism: An Integrated Study*, New York: St. Martin's Press, 1988, page 355. Source of Watson remark: Detlefsen, Robert R., "White Like Me," *The New Republic*, April 10, 1989, page 18.

448. Clines, Francis X., "What's 3 Letters and Zoologically Incorrect?", *The New York Times*, February 4, 1993, page A1.

449. Kramarae, Cheris, and Treichler, Paula A., *A Feminist Dictionary*, Boston: Pandora Press, 1985, page 487.

450. Pellow-McCauley, Theresa, cited in Baron, Dennis, *Grammar and Gender*, New Haven, Yale University Press, 1986, page 149.

451. "Words We Love to Hate," *The Disability Rag*, Winter 1990, pages 13–15.

452. Goldfield, Bina, *The Efemcipated English Handbook*, New York: Westover Press, 1983, page 119.

453. Frank, Francine Wattman, and Treichler, Paula A., *Language, Gender and Professional Writing: Theoretical Approaches and Guidelines for Nonsexist Usage*, New York: Modern Language Association, 1989, page 200.

454. Walker, Alice, quoted in Frank, Francine Wattman, and Treichler, Paula A.,

Language, Gender and Professional Writing: Theoretical Approaches and Guidelines for Nonsexist Usage, New York: Modern Language Association, 1989, page 203.

455. Baron, Dennis, *Grammar and Gender,* New Haven, Yale University Press, 1986, page 183.

456. Spender, Dr. Dale, *Man Made Language,* London: Pandora Press, 1990, page 181.

457. Alicen, Debbie, "Intertextuality: The Language of Lesbian Relationships," *Trivia,* Fall 1983, page 6, as cited in Kramarae, Cheris, and Treichler, Paula A., *A Feminist Dictionary,* Boston: Pandora Press, 1985, page 505.

458. *Random House Webster's College Dictionary,* New York: Random House, 1991, page 1532; and Pellow-McCauley, Theresa, cited in Baron, Dennis, *Grammar and Gender,* New Haven, Yale University Press, 1986, page 149.

459. Daly, Mary, *Gyn/Ecology,* Boston: Beacon Press, 1978, page 85.

PART II: POLITICALLY INCORRECT/ POLITICALLY CORRECT DICTIONARY

Source information for most of the items in Part II can be found by consulting the corresponding entry in Part I, "A Dictionary of Politically Correct (PC) Terms and Phrases." When terms or quotations presented in Part II do not appear elsewhere in the book, source references are provided here.

1. The American Hyphen Society.

2. Hirsch, Barbara B., *Divorce: What a Woman Needs to Know,* Chicago: Henry Regnery, page 138.

3. Sorrels, Bobbye D., *The Nonsexist Communicator: Solving the Problems of Gender and Awkwardness in Modern English,* Englewood Cliffs, NJ: Prentice Hall, 1983, page 124.

4. The Department of Rhetoric, University of California at Berkeley, 1991 handout.

5. Rothenberg, Paula S., *Racism and Sexism: An Integrated Study,* New York: St. Martin's Press, 1988, page 271.

6. Mayer, Milton, "On the Siblinghood of Persons," *The Progressive,* number 39, 1975, reprinted in Baron, Dennis, *Grammar and Gender,* New Haven: Yale University Press, 1986, page 207.

7. Mayer, Milton, "On the Siblinghood of Persons," *The Progressive,* number 39, 1975, reprinted in Baron, Dennis, *Grammar and Gender,* New Haven: Yale University Press, 1986, page 207.

8. Defined by Ann Ferguson in "Androgyny As an Ideal for Human Development," anthologized in Rothenberg, Paula S., *Racism and Sexism: An Integrated Study,* New York: St. Martin's Press, 1988, page 369.

9. Lapham, Lewis H., "Acceptable Opinions," *Harper's Magazine,* December 1990.

10. Lutz, William, *Doublespeak,* New York: Harper Perennial, 1990, page 145.

11. Black, George, "Briefingspeak," anthologized in Sifry, Micah, and Cerf, Christopher, *The Gulf War Reader,* New York: Times Books/Random House, 1991, page 389.

12. The American Hyphen Society.

13. Washburn, Andrew J., quoted in *The Disability Rag,* Winter 1990, page 14.

14. Lutz, William, "Doublespeak in Education," *Education Week,* November 29, 1989.

15. Pei, Mario, *Double-Speak in America*, New York: Hawthorn Books, 1973, page 142.

16. Lutz, William, *Doublespeak*, New York: Harper Perennial, 1990, page 109.

17. *Dictionary of Cautionary Words and Phrases,* compiled by the 1989 Multicultural Management Program Fellows of the University of Missouri Journalism School.

18. Fury, Kathleen, "A Generous Fit," *New Woman,* February 1991, page 38.

19. Lutz, William, *Doublespeak,* New York: Harper Perennial, 1990, page 61.

20. The Department of Rhetoric, University of California at Berkeley, 1991 handout.

21. The Department of Rhetoric, University of California at Berkeley, 1991 handout.

22. A term used by *USA Today* to describe William "Refrigerator" Perry of the Chicago Bears, cited in *The Quarterly Review of Doublespeak,* a publication of the National Council of Teachers of English, Urbana, Illinois, January 1989, page 9.

23. Kramarae, Cheris, and Treichler, Paula A., *A Feminist Dictionary,* Boston: Pandora Press, 1985, page 155.

24. U.S. Department of Labor, *Job Title Revisions to Eliminate Sex- and Age-Referent Language from the Dictionary of Occupational Titles,* Washington, D.C., 1975, page 34.

25. The Department of Rhetoric, University of California at Berkeley, 1991 handout.

26. Goddard, Robert W., "Use Language Effectively," *Personnel Journal,* April 1989, page 32.

27. Lennert, Midge, and Willson, Norma, *A Woman's New World Dictionary,* Lomita, CA: 51% Publications, 1973, page 5; Kramarae, Cheris, and Treichler, Paula A., *A Feminist Dictionary,* Boston: Pandora Press, 1985, page 176.

28. Rawson, Hugh, *A Dictionary of Euphemisms and Other Doubletalk,* New York: Crown Publishers, 1981, page 291.

29. Warland, Betsy, *Proper Deafinitions,* Vancouver: Press Gang Publishers, 1990, page 70.

30. *Dictionary of Cautionary Words and Phrases,* compiled by the 1989 Multicultural Management Program Fellows of the University of Missouri Journalism School.

31. The American Hyphen Society.

32. The American Hyphen Society.

33. OED, reprinted in Baron, Dennis, *Grammar and Gender,* New Haven: Yale University Press, 1986, page 180.

34. *The Quarterly Review of Doublespeak,* a publication of the National Council of Teachers of English, Urbana, Illinois, April 1991, page 3.

35. The American Hyphen Society.

36. *Dictionary of Cautionary Words and Phrases,* compiled by the 1989 Multicultural Management Project Fellows of the University of Missouri Journalism School.

37. Three Rivers, Amoja, *Cultural Etiquette: A Guide for the Well-Intentioned,* Indian Valley, Virginia: Market Wimmin, 1990, page 10.

38. Matthews, Anne, "Brave, New 'Cruelty Free' World," *The New York Times,* July 7, 1991.

39. Leo, John, "The new verbal order," *U.S. News & World Report,* July 22, 1991, page 14.

40. The American Hyphen Society.

41. The American Hyphen Society.

42. *Dictionary of Cautionary Words and Phrases,* compiled by the 1989 Multicultural Management Program Fellows of the University of Missouri Journalism School.

43. Rees, Nigel, *The Politically Correct Phrasebook*, London: Bloomsbury, 1993, page 82.

44. The American Hyphen Society.

45. The American Hyphen Society.

46. Berg, Ellen, "Feminist Theory: Moving Sociology from the Malestream," *Footnotes,* March 1987, page 5.

47. Dumond, Val, *The Elements of Nonsexist Usage,* New York: Prentice Hall, 1990, page 82.

48. Dworkin, Andrea, *Our Blood: Prophecies and Discourses on Sexual Politics,* New York: Harper & Row, 1976, page 27 .

49. Spender, Dale, *Women of Ideas and What Men Have Done to Them,* London: Routledge and Kegan Paul, 1982, page 341.

50. McCarthy, Colman, "Euphemistic Language Makes the Gruesome Palatable," *The Washington Post,* 1990 column, reprinted in *The Quarterly Review of Doublespeak,* a publication of the National Council of Teachers of English, Urbana, Illinois, July 1990, page 7.

51. McKenna, Chris, "Regents OK Writing History Books," *New York Post,* Friday, July 26, 1991.

52. Smith, Jack, "Clearly, It's a Plastic Language With Devious Overtones," *Los Angeles Times,* October 24, 1990, page E6.

53. Suggested by American Hyphen Society psycholinguist Sarah Bruce Durkee.

54. *Dictionary of Cautionary Words and Phrases,* compiled by the 1989 Multicultural Management Program Fellows of the University of Missouri Journalism School.

55. The American Hyphen Society.

56. "Definitions," handout published by the Smith College Office of Student Affairs, 1990; Leo, John, "The new verbal order," *U.S. News & World Report,* July 22, 1991, page 14.

57. The American Hyphen Society.

58. The American Hyphen Society.

59. Gusewelle, C. W., "Perils Still Abound—Only Their Names Are Gentler," article in *The Kansas City Star,* reprinted in *The Quarterly Review of Doublespeak,* a publication of the National Council of Teachers of English, Urbana, Illinois, July 1990, page 8.

60. The American Hyphen Society.

61. The American Hyphen Society.

62. Landers, Ann, syndicated column, October 20, 1988, cited in *The Quarterly Review of Doublespeak,* a publication of the National Council of Teachers of English, Urbana, Illinois, July 1989, page 10.

63. The Department of Rhetoric, University of California at Berkeley, 1991 handout.

64. Neaman, Judith S., and Silver, Carole G., *Kind Words,* New York: Avon Books, 1991, page 146.

65. Daly, Mary, *Gyn/Ecology,* Boston: Beacon Press, 1978, page 8.

66. The American Hyphen Society, with special thanks to lifestyle consultants Robin Batteau, David Buskin, and Norman Stiles.

67. Neaman, Judith S., and Silver, Carole G., *Kind Words,* New York: Avon Books, 1991, page 299.

68. Burns, Rick, "A Soccer Coach's Lament About His Sensitive Team," *The NCAA News,* November 18, 1991, excerpted in *Harper's,* September 1992, pages 22-23.

69. Capek, Mary Ellen S., *A Woman's Thesaurus,* New York: Harper & Row, 1987, page 461.

70. *The New York Times,* March 22, 1991, reprinted in *The Quarterly Review of Doublespeak,* a publication of the National Council of Teachers of English, Urbana, Illinois, April 1991, page 9.

71. Moore, Robert B., "Racist Stereotyping in the English Language," reprinted in Rothenberg, Paula S., *Racism and Sexism: An Integrated Study,* New York: St. Martin's Press, 1988, page 276.

72. Source of "indefinitely idled" and "in an orderly transition between career

changes": Lutz, William, *Doublespeak,* New York: Harper Perennial, 1990, pages 127, 133.

73. The American Hyphen Society.

74. The American Hyphen Society.

75. Collins, Patricia, and Anderson, Margaret, editors, *An Inclusive Curriculum: Race, Class and Gender in Sociological Instruction,* Washington, D.C.: The American Sociological Association, 1987.

76. Smith, Barbara, "Notes for Yet Another Paper on Black Feminism," quoted in Kramarae, Cheris, and Treichler, Paula A., *A Feminist Dictionary,* Boston: Pandora Press, 1985, page 483.

77. Dumond, Val, *Elements of Nonsexist Usage,* New York: Prentice Hall Press, 1990, page 46.

78. Quoted in Lutz, William, *Doublespeak,* New York: Harper Perennial, 1990, page 106.

79. The American Hyphen Society.

80. Clines, Francis X., "What's 3 Letters and Zoologically Incorrect?", *The New York Times,* February 4, 1993, pages A1, B4.

81. Rose, Barbara, Letter to *The New York Times Magazine,* March 14, 1993.

PART III: OTHER SUSPECT WORDS, CONCEPTS, AND "HEROES"
TO BE AVOIDED AND/OR DISCARDED

1. Kimball, Roger, *Tenured Radicals,* New York: Harper Perennial, 1991, page 168.

2. *The Washington Post,* February 8, 1991, page A19.

3. *The Champaign-Urbana News Gazette,* February 19, 1989, quoted in *The Quarterly Review of Doublespeak,* a publication of the National Council of Teachers of English, Urbana, Illinois, July 1991, page 2.

4. Schleifer, Harriet, "Images of Death and Life," and Regan, Tom, "The Case for Animal Rights," both anthologized in Singer, Peter, *In Defense of Animals,* New York, Harper Perennial Library, 1985, pages 72, 14, 26.

5. Amylee, "How Not to Talk to an Indian," originally published in *The Pathfinder Directory* of the Native American Resource Center, and reprinted in Three Rivers, Amoja, *Cultural Etiquette: A Guide for the Well-Intentioned,* Indian Valley, Virginia: Market Wimmin, 1990, page 20.

6. Zalk, Sue Rosenberg, "Men in the Academy: A Psychological Profile of Harassment," anthologized in Paludi, Michele A., *Ivory Power: Sexual Harassment on Campus,* Albany: State University of New York Press, 1990, page 150.

7. Daly, Mary, *Gyn/Ecology,* Boston: Beacon Press, 1978, pages 86n, 105.

8. Singer, Peter, *Animal Liberation,* New York, Avon Books, 1990, page 187.

9. D'Souza, Dinesh, *Illiberal Education: The Politics of Race and Sex on Campus,* New York: Free Press, 1991, page 181.

10. Hartman, Geoffrey, *Saving the Text: Literature/Derrida/Philosophy,* Baltimore: Johns Hopkins University Press, 1984, pages 60–61.

11. *Stanford Daily,* April 22, 1988.

12. Taylor, John, "Are You Politically Correct?" *New York,* January 21, 1991, page 36.

13. Kimball, Roger, *Tenured Radicals,* New York: Harper Perennial, 1991, page 10.

14. Kramarae, Cheris, and Treichler, Paula A., *A Feminist Dictionary,* Boston: Pandora Press, 1985, pages 115–16.

15. Firestone, Shulamith, *The Dialectic of Sex: The Case for Feminine Revolution,* New York, William Morrow, 1970, page 233. Quoted in: Kramarae, Cheris, and Treichler, Paula A., *A Feminist Dictionary,* Boston: Pandora Press, 1985.

16. Traub, James, "Back to Basic," *The New Republic,* February 8. 1993, page 19.

17. Taylor, John, "Are You Politically Correct?" *New York,* January 21, 1991, page 38.

18. Kimball, Roger, *Tenured Radicals,* New York: Harper Perennial, 1991, page 68.

19. Leo, John, "A political correctness roundup," *U.S. News & World Report,* June 22, 1992, page 31.

20. Levy, Jacob, "The Ennui of 'P.C.,'" *Brown Alumni Monthly,* October 1991; *Newsweek,* December 24, 1990, page 51.

21. Asante, Molefi Kete, *Afrocentricity,* Trenton, NJ: Africa World Press, 1988, page 89.

22. Daly, Mary, *Websters' First New Intergalactic Wickedary of the English Language,* Boston: Beacon Press, 1987, page 187.

23. Leo, John, "PC follies: The year in review," *U.S. News & World Report,* January 27, 1992, page 22.

24. Warland, Betsy, *Proper Deafinitions,* Vancouver: Press Gang Publishers, 1990, page 70.

25. *Newsweek,* December 24, 1990, page 51.

26. Henley, Nancy, *Body Politics,* Englewood Cliffs, NJ: Prentice Hall, 1977, page 10. Quoted in: Kramarae, Cheris, and Treichler, Paula A., *A Feminist Dictionary,* Boston: Pandora Press, 1985.

27. Taylor, John, "Are You Politically Correct?," *New York,* January 21, 1991, page 35.

28. Dworkin, Andrea, quoted in Leo, John, "The words of the culture war," *U.S. News & World Report,* October 28, 1991, page 31.

29. Detlefsen, Robert R., "White Like Me," *The New Republic,* April 10, 1989, page 19.

30. D'Souza, Dinesh, *Illiberal Education,* Free Press, 1991, pages 222–23.

31. Beers, David, "PC? B.S.," *Mother Jones,* September/October 1991, page 65.

32. Leo, John, "A political correctness roundup," *U.S. News & World Report*, June 22, 1992, page 31.

33. Three Rivers, Amoja, *Cultural Etiquette: A Guide for the Well-Intentioned*, Indian Valley, Virginia: Market Wimmin, 1990, page 5.

34. Frye, Marilyn, "Oppression," anthologized in Rothenberg, Paula S., *Racism and Sexism: An Integrated Study*, New York: St. Martin's Press, 1988, page 41.

35. Taylor, John, "Men on Trial," *New York*, December 16, 1991, page 34.

36. Dworkin, Andrea, *Our Blood: Prophecies and Discourses on Sexual Politics*, New York: Harper & Row, 1976, page 27, and Spender, Dale, *Women of Ideas and What Men Have Done to Them*, London: Routledge and Kegan Paul, 1982, page 341.

37. Adler, Jerry, et al., "African Dreams," *Newsweek*, September 23, 1991, page 44.

38. D'Souza, Dinesh, *Illiberal Education: The Politics of Race and Sex on Campus*, New York: The Free Press, 1991, page 189.

39. Adler, Jerry, "Taking Offense," *Newsweek*, December 24, 1990, page 51.

40. Phillips, Lisa, "No Man's Land: At the Threshold of a Millennium," *1993 Biennial Exhibition*, catalog, New York: Whitney Museum of American Art in Association with Harry N. Abrams, Inc., 1993, pages 53-54.

41. Ferguson, Ann, "Androgyny As an Ideal for Human Development," reprinted in Rothenberg, Paula S., *Racism and Sexism: An Integrated Study*, New York: St. Martin's Press, 1988, pages 369–70.

42. Three Rivers, Amoja, *Cultural Etiquette: A Guide for the Well-Intentioned*, Indian Valley, Virginia: Market Wimmin, 1990, page 16.

43. Henry, William A., III, "Upside Down in the Groves of Academe," *Time*, April 1, 1991, page 66.

44. Lorde, Audre, "Age, Race, Class and Sex: Women Redefining Difference," a paper delivered at the Copeland Colloquium, Amherst College, April 1980, and reprinted in Rothenberg, Paula S., *Racism and Sexism: An Integrated Study*, New York: St. Martin's Press, 1988, pages 353–54.

45. D'Souza, Dinesh, *Illiberal Education*, Free Press, 1991, pages 6–7.

46. "How to Speak Post-Modern, Being a Glossary of Actual Post-Modern Terminology in Current Usage Made Sensible for the Un/informed and Semi(initiated), Drawn from the book *Post-Modernism and the Social Sciences* by Pauline Marie Rosenau," pamphlet, Princeton, New Jersey: Princeton University Press, 1991.

47. Zalk, Sue Rosenberg, "Men in the Academy," anthologized in Paludi, Michele A., *Ivory Power: Sexual Harassment on Campus*, Albany: State University of New York Press, 1990, pages 142–55.

48. Taylor, John, "Are You Politically Correct?," *New York*, January 21, 1991, page 38.

49. Traub, James, "Back to Basic," *The New Republic*, February 8, 1993, pages 18-19.

50. Leo, John, "PC follies: The year in review," *U.S. News & World Report*, January 27, 1992, page 26.

51. *Dictionary of Cautionary Words and Phrases,* compiled by the Multicultural Management Program Fellows of the University of Missouri Journalism School, 1989.

52. "Who Needs the Great Works?" forum, *Harper's Magazine,* September 1989, page 46.

53. Koss, Mary P., "Changed Lives: The Psychological Impact of Sexual Harassment," anthologized in Paludi, Michele A., *Ivory Power: Sexual Harassment on Campus,* Albany: State University of New York Press, 1990, page 75.

54. Fausto-Sterling, Anne, "How Many Sexes Are There?", *The New York Times,* March 12, 1993, page A29.

55. Taylor, John, "Are You Politically Correct?," *New York,* January 21, 1991, pages 39–40.

56. "How to Speak Post-Modern, Being a Glossary of Actual Post-Modern Terminology in Current Usage Made Sensible for the Un/informed and Semi(initiated), Drawn from the Book *Post-Modernism and the Social Sciences* by Pauline Marie Rosenau," pamphlet, Princeton, New Jersey: Princeton University Press, 1991.

57. Ozersky, Josh, "The Enlightenment Theology of Political Correctness," *Tikkun,* July/August 1991, page 37.

58. Stanley, Julia Penelope, and Robbins, Susan W., "One of Our Agents Is Missing," essay cited in Frank, Francine Wattman, and Treichler, Paula A., *Language, Gender and Professional Writing,* New York: The Modern Language Association, 1989, page 222.

59. Stanley, Julia Penelope, quoted in Kramarae, Cheris, and Treichler, Paula A., *A Feminist Dictionary,* Boston: Pandora Press, 1985, page 38.

60. Greenblatt, Stephen, "Fiction and Friction," quoted in Kimball, Roger, *Tenured Radicals,* New York: Harper Perennial, 1991, page 49.

61. Frank, Francine Wattman, and Treichler, Paula A., *Language, Gender and Professional Writing: Theoretical Approaches and Guidelines for Nonsexist Usage,* New York: Modern Language Association, 1989, page 201.

62. Three Rivers, Amoja, *Cultural Etiquette: A Guide for the Well-Intentioned,* Indian Valley, Virginia: Market Wimmin, 1990, page 16.

63. Leo, John, "PC follies: The year in review," *U.S. News & World Report,* January 27, 1992, page 26.

PART IV: KNOW YOUR OPPRESSOR: A BILINGUAL GLOSSARY OF BUREAUCRATICALLY SUITABLE (BS) LANGUAGE

1. Rawson, Hugh, *A Dictionary of Euphemisms and Other Doubletalk,* New York: Crown Publishers, 1981, page 12.

2. Dickson, Paul, *Slang!,* New York: Pocket Books, 1990, page 46.

3. *The Quarterly Review of Doublespeak,* a publication of the National Council of Teachers of English, Urbana, Illinois, July 1991, page 2.

4. Lutz, William, *Doublespeak,* New York: Harper Perennial, 1990, page 176.

5. Neaman, Judith S., and Silver, Carole G., *Kind Words,* New York: Avon Books, 1991, page 351.

6. Lutz, William, *Doublespeak,* New York: Harper Perennial, 1990, page 222.

7. Fahey, Tom, *The Joys of Jargon,* New York: Barron's, 1990, page 123.

8. Rawson, Hugh, *A Dictionary of Euphemisms and Other Doubletalk,* New York: Crown Publishers, 1981, page 20.

9. Lutz, William, "Fourteen Years of Doublespeak," *English Journal,* March 1988, page 41.

10. Rawson, Hugh, *A Dictionary of Euphemisms and Other Doubletalk,* New York: Crown Publishers, 1981, page 27.

11. *Nova,* PBS television special on the incident at Chernobyl, Autumn 1991.

12. Lutz, William, *Doublespeak,* New York: Harper Perennial, 1990, page 129.

13. Smith, Jack, "Clearly, It's a Plastic Language With Devious Overtones," *Los Angeles Times,* October 24, 1990, page E6.

14. Fahey, Tom, *The Joys of Jargon,* New York: Barron's, 1990, page 123.

15. Black, George, "Briefingspeak," anthologized in Sifry, Micah, and Cerf, Christopher, *The Gulf War Reader,* New York: Times Books/Random House, 1991, page 390.

16. Lutz, William, *Doublespeak,* New York: Harper Perennial, 1990, page 215.

17. Wooten, Jim, Report broadcast on *The World News Tonight,* ABC Television News, February 17, 1993.

18. The National Transportation Safety Board, quoted in Lutz, William, *Doublespeak,* New York: Harper Perennial, 1990, page 213.

19. Rawson, Hugh, *A Dictionary of Euphemisms and Other Doubletalk,* New York: Crown Publishers, 1981, page 61.

20. Dickson, Paul, *Slang!,* New York: Pocket Books, 1990, page 47.

21. NASA, after the *Challenger* incident, quoted in Lutz, William, *Doublespeak,* New York: Harper Perennial, 1990, page 223.

22. *Executive Recruiter News,* Fitzwilliam, New Hampshire, November 1990.

23. *Conservative Chronicle,* April 17, 1991, page 21, as cited in *The Quarterly Review of Doublespeak,* April 1991, page 9.

24. Lutz, William, "Doublespeak in Education," *Education Week,* November 29, 1989.

25. Lutz, William, *Doublespeak,* New York: Harper Perennial, 1990, page 213.

26. Philadelphia hospital, quoted by Lutz, William, *Doublespeak,* New York: Harper Perennial, 1990, page 67.

27. Fahey, Tom, *The Joys of Jargon,* New York: Barron's, 1990, page 123.

28. Hawkins, Arthur H., *Self-Discipline in Labor-Management Relations.* Quoted in Pei, Mario, *Double-Speak in America,* New York: Hawthorn Books, 1973, page 137.

29. *Executive Recruiter News,* Fitzwilliam, New Hampshire, November 1990.

30. *The Wall Street Journal,* March 19, 1991, cited in *The Quarterly Review of Doublespeak,* a publication of the National Council of Teachers of English, Urbana, Illinois, April 1991, page 1.

31. Neaman, Judith S., and Silver, Carole G., *Kind Words,* New York: Avon Books, 1991, page 321.

32. Neaman, Judith S., and Silver, Carole G., *Kind Words,* New York: Avon Books, 1991, page 337.

33. Lutz, William, *Doublespeak,* New York: Harper Perennial, 1990, page 176.

34. Lutz, William, *Doublespeak,* New York: Harper Perennial, 1990, page 105.

35. Nuclear Regulatory Commission spokesperson describing the Three Mile Island anomaly.

36. Rawson, Hugh, *A Dictionary of Euphemisms and Other Doubletalk,* New York: Crown Publishers, 1981, page 91.

37. Neaman, Judith S., and Silver, Carole G., *Kind Words,* New York: Avon Books, 1991, page 335.

38. Lutz, William, *Doublespeak,* New York: Harper Perennial, 1990, page 66.

39. The National Transportation Safety Board, quoted in Lutz, William, *Doublespeak,* New York: Harper Perennial, 1990, page 213.

40. Rawson, Hugh, *A Dictionary of Euphemisms and Other Doubletalk,* New York: Crown Publishers, 1981.

41. *The Quarterly Review of Doublespeak,* a publication of the National Council of Teachers of English, Urbana, Illinois, July 1991, page 2.

42. Lutz, William, *Doublespeak,* New York: Harper Perennial, 1990.

43. Lutz, William, *Doublespeak,* New York: Harper Perennial, 1990, pages 104–5.

44. Commager, Henry S., "The Defeat of America," *New York Review of Books,* October 5, 1972, page 10.

45. Rawson, Hugh, *A Dictionary of Euphemisms and Other Doubletalk,* New York: Crown Publishers, 1981, page 119.

46. *The San Francisco Chronicle,* May 25, 1989, as cited in *The Quarterly Review of Doublespeak,* a publication of the National Council of Teachers of English, Urbana, Illinois, October 1989, page 5.

47. *The Quarterly Review of Doublespeak,* a publication of the National Council of Teachers of English, Urbana, Illinois, April 1990, page 2.

48. Allan, Keith, and Burridge, Kate, *Euphemism and Dysphemism,* New York: Oxford University Press, 1991, page 169.

49. Leo, John, "Translations from the Journalese," *Washington Post* article reprinted in *The Quarterly Review of Doublespeak,* a publication of the National Council of Teachers of English, Urbana, Illinois, January 1991, page 11.

50. Rawson, Hugh, *A Dictionary of Euphemisms and Other Doubletalk,* New York: Crown Publishers, 1981, page 132.

51. Rawson, Hugh, *A Dictionary of Euphemisms and Other Doubletalk,* New York: Crown Publishers, 1981, pages 91–92.

52. Nemy, Enid, "What's Said Isn't Always What's Meant," 1988 article in *The New York Times,* reprinted in *The Quarterly Review of Doublespeak,* a publication of the National Council of Teachers of English, Urbana, Illinois, July 1990, page 12.

53. *The Quarterly Review of Doublespeak,* a publication of the National Council of Teachers of English, Urbana, Illinois, July 1989, page 10.

54. Trowbridge, T. R., III, "On Euphemisms—Or, Through the Dark, Glassily," *The New York Times,* September 21, 1988, reprinted in *The Quarterly Review of Doublespeak,* a publication of the National Council of Teachers of English, Urbana, Illinois, April 1989, page 9.

55. Lutz, William, *Doublespeak,* New York: Harper Perennial, 1990, page 66.

56. Black, George, "Briefingspeak," anthologized in Sifry, Micah, and Cerf, Christopher, *The Gulf War Reader,* New York: Times Books/Random House, 1991.

57. *Executive Recruiter News,* Fitzwilliam, New Hampshire, November 1990.

58. Rawson, Hugh, *A Dictionary of Euphemisms and Other Doubletalk,* New York: Crown Publishers, 1981, page 146.

59. Lutz, William, "Doublespeak in Education," *Education Week,* November 29, 1989.

60. Lutz, William, "Doublespeak in Education," *Education Week,* November 29, 1989.

61. *The Quarterly Review of Doublespeak,* a publication of the National Council of Teachers of English, Urbana, Illinois, July 1991, page 1.

62. Wooten, Jim, Report broadcast on *The World News Tonight,* ABC Television News, February 17, 1993.

63. Lutz, William, *Doublespeak,* New York: Harper Perennial, 1990, page 4.

64. *The Quarterly Review of Doublespeak,* a publication of the National Council of Teachers of English, Urbana, Illinois, July 1991, page 2.

65. Neaman, Judith S., and Silver, Carole G., *Kind Words,* New York: Avon Books, 1991, page 334.

66. Lutz, William, *Doublespeak,* New York: Harper Perennial, 1990, page 128.

67. *The Philadelphia Inquirer,* June 16, 1989, page 10-D. As cited in *The Quarterly Review of Doublespeak,* a publication of the National Council of Teachers of English, Urbana, Illinois, October 1989, page 5.

68. Lutz, William, *Doublespeak,* New York: Harper Perennial, 1990, page 114.

69. Lutz, William, *Doublespeak,* New York: Harper Perennial, 1990, page 63.

70. Lutz, William, *Doublespeak,* New York: Harper Perennial, 1990, page 128.

71. Lutz, William, *Doublespeak,* New York: Harper Perennial, 1990, page 67.

72. Rawson, Hugh, *A Dictionary of Euphemisms and Other Doubletalk,* New York: Crown Publishers, 1981, page 4.

73. Black, George, "Briefingspeak," anthologized in Sifry, Micah, and Cerf, Christopher, *The Gulf War Reader,* New York: Times Books/Random House, 1991.

74. Hawkins, Arthur H., *Self-Discipline in Labor-Management Relations,* quoted in Pei, Mario, *Double-Speak in America,* Hawthorn Books, 1973, page 137.

75. *The Quarterly Review of Doublespeak,* a publication of the National Council of Teachers of English, Urbana, Illinois, April 1991, page 9.

76. *The Quarterly Review of Doublespeak,* a publication of the National Council of Teachers of English, Urbana, Illinois, April 1990, page 7.

77. Lutz, William, *Doublespeak,* New York: Harper Perennial, 1990, page 114.

78. School board in Cleveland, Ohio, 1982. Cited in Lutz, William, "Doublespeak in Education," *Education Week,* November 29, 1989.

79. Lutz, William, *Doublespeak,* New York: Harper Perennial, 1990, page 145.

80. Greenfield, Meg, "Why Nothing Is 'Wrong' Anymore," *Newsweek,* July 28, 1986, page 72.

81. *The Quarterly Review of Doublespeak,* a publication of the National Council of Teachers of English, Urbana, Illinois, January 1991, page 1.

82. *Executive Recruiter News,* Fitzwilliam, New Hampshire, November 1990.

83. Neaman, Judith S., and Silver, Carole G., *Kind Words,* New York: Avon Books, 1991, page 324.

84. Lutz, William, *Doublespeak,* New York: Harper Perennial, 1990, page 106.

85. Neaman, Judith S., and Silver, Carole G., *Kind Words,* New York: Avon Books, 1991, page 334.

86. Fahey, Tom, *The Joys of Jargon,* New York: Barron's, 1990, page 123.

87. Lutz, William, *Doublespeak,* New York: Harper Perennial, 1990, page 176.

88. Pei, Mario, *Double-Speak in America,* New York: Hawthorn Books, 1973, page 99.

89. Defined by Don Ethan Miller in *The Book of Jargon.* Cited in Dickson, Paul, *Slang!,* New York: Pocket Books, 1990, page 51.

90. Lutz, William, *Doublespeak,* New York: Harper Perennial, 1990, page 219.

91. Neaman, Judith S., and Silver, Carole G., *Kind Words,* New York: Avon Books, 1991, page 337.

92. Smith, Jack, "Clearly, It's a Plastic Language With Devious Overtones," *Los Angeles Times,* October 24, 1990, page E6.

93. Lutz, William, *Doublespeak,* New York: Harper Perennial, 1990, page 127.

94. Dickson, Paul, *Slang!,* New York: Pocket Books, 1990, page 51.

95. *Executive Recruiter News,* Fitzwilliam, New Hampshire, November 1990.

96. *Sludge,* a biweekly newsletter of the wastewater industry, December 5, 1990, page 198. As cited in *The Quarterly Review of Doublespeak,* a publication of the National Council of Teachers of English, Urbana, Illinois, April 1991, page 7.

97. Convicted insider trader Dennis Levine, as quoted by Norris, Floyd, "Market Watch," *The New York Times,* September 22, 1991.

98. LeMay, Harold, Lerner, Sid, and Taylor, Marian, *The New Words Dictionary,* New York: Ballantine Books, 1988, page 37.

99. Dickson, Paul, *Slang!,* New York: Pocket Books, 1990, page 52.

100. Rawson, Hugh, *A Dictionary of Euphemisms and Other Doubletalk,* New York: Crown Publishers, 1981, page 237.

101. *The Wall Street Journal,* March 19, 1991, cited in *The Quarterly Review of Doublespeak,* a publication of the National Council of Teachers of English, Urbana, Illinois, April 1991, page 1.

102. Rawson, Hugh, *A Dictionary of Euphemisms and Other Doubletalk,* New York: Crown Publishers, 1981, page 238.

103. Wooten, Jim, Report broadcast on *The World News Tonight,* ABC Television News, February 17, 1993.

104. Rawson, Hugh, *A Dictionary of Euphemisms and Other Doubletalk,* New York: Crown Publishers, 1981, page 245.

105. Lutz, William, *Doublespeak,* New York: Harper Perennial, 1990, page 233.

106. Dickson, Paul, *Slang!,* New York: Pocket Books, 1990, page 167.

107. Rawson, Hugh, *A Dictionary of Euphemisms and Other Doubletalk,* New York: Crown Publishers, 1981, page 248.

108. Rawson, Hugh, *A Dictionary of Euphemisms and Other Doubletalk,* New York: Crown Publishers, 1981.

109. Lutz, William, *Doublespeak,* New York: Harper Perennial, 1990, page 178.

110. *Executive Recruiter News,* Fitzwilliam, New Hampshire, November 1990.

111. Smith, Jack, "Clearly, It's a Plastic Language With Devious Overtones," *Los Angeles Times,* October 24, 1990, page E6.

112. *College English,* January 1990, page 50.

113. Rawson, Hugh, *A Dictionary of Euphemisms and Other Doubletalk,* New York: Crown Publishers, 1981, page 263.

114. Rawson, Hugh, *A Dictionary of Euphemisms and Other Doubletalk,* New York: Crown Publishers, 1981, page 263.

115. Lutz, William, *Doublespeak,* New York: Harper Perennial, 1990, page 108.

116. Neaman, Judith S., and Silver, Carole G., *Kind Words,* New York: Avon Books, 1991, page 334.

117. *The Wall Street Journal,* March 19, 1991, cited in *The Quarterly Review of Doublespeak,* a publication of the National Council of Teachers of English, Urbana, Illinois, April 1991, page 1.

118. Lutz, William, *Doublespeak,* New York: Harper Perennial, 1990, page 269.

119. "English: It's Abused in Business," *The Atlanta Journal and Constitution,* May 7, 1990, page D-8.

120. Dickson, Paul, *Slang!,* New York: Pocket Books, 1990, page 52.

121. Lutz, William, "Doublespeak in Education," *Education Week*, November 29, 1989.

122. Rawson, Hugh, *A Dictionary of Euphemisms and Other Doubletalk,* New York: Crown Publishers, 1981, page 12.

123. Lutz, William, *Doublespeak,* New York: Harper Perennial, 1990, page 19.

124. Wooten, Jim, Report broadcast on *The World News Tonight,* ABC Television News, February 17, 1993.

125. Leo, John, "The new verbal order," *U.S. News & World Report,* July 22, 1991, page 14.

126. *The Quarterly Review of Doublespeak,* a publication of the National Council of Teachers of English, Urbana, Illlinois, April 1991, page 6.

127. Lutz, William, *Doublespeak,* New York: Harper Perennial, 1990, page 67.

128. Allan, Keith, and Burridge, Kate, *Euphemism and Dysphemism,* New York: Oxford University Press, 1991, page 168.

129. Fahey, Tom, *The Joys of Jargon,* New York: Barron's, 1990, page 123.

130. Black, George, "Briefingspeak," anthologized in Sifry, Micah, and Cerf, Christopher, *The Gulf War Reader,* New York: Times Books/Random House, 1991, page 390.

131. Mitford, Jessica, *Kind and Unusual Punishment: The Prison Business,* as quoted in Rawson, Hugh, *A Dictionary of Euphemisms and Other Doubletalk,* New York: Crown Publishers, 1981.

132. U.S. Secretary of Energy Donald Hodel, as quoted in Lutz, William, *Doublespeak,* New York: Harper Perennial, 1990, page 213.

133. Lutz, William, *Doublespeak,* New York: Harper Perennial, 1990, page 213.

134. *The Quarterly Review of Doublespeak,* a publication of the National Council of Teachers of English, Urbana, Illlinois, October 1989, page 4.

135. "NCTE to You," *College English,* January 1990, page 50.

136. Lutz, William, *Doublespeak,* New York: Harper Perennial, 1990, page 213.

137. Lutz, William, *Doublespeak,* New York: Harper Perennial, 1990, page 119.

138. *The Quarterly Review of Doublespeak,* a publication of the National Council of Teachers of English, Urbana, Illlinois, July 1991, page 1.

139. Pick, John, *The Modern Newspeak,* London: Harrap, 1984, page 60.

140. Lutz, William, *Doublespeak,* New York: Harper Perennial, 1990.

ACKNOWLEDGMENTS

The Official Politically Correct Dictionary and Handbook owes its existence to the contributions of many people—friends, colleagues, and writers and scholars whose work preceded ours. To paraphrase Sir Isaac Newton, "If we have seen further, it is by standing on the shoulders of heightism survivors."

First and foremost, we wish to thank the American Hyphen Society and its Research-and-Development Task Force cochairs, Karen Larsen Meizels, Rebecca Beuchler, Maryam Mohit, and Ann Toner. The society's network of linguistics consultants also provided many invaluable suggestions; in particular, we're grateful to Jane Aaron, Skip Blumberg, Michael Chambers, Gwyneth Jones Cravens, Sarah Durkee, Rosa Ehrenreich (who took time off from her nurturing work with the Big Sibling Movement to contribute to our project), Craig Lambert, Juliet Mohit, Arlene Sherman, Micah Sifry, and Norman Stiles.

Pioneering works by Jerry Adler, the Department of Rhetoric of the University of California at Berkeley, Bina Goldfield, Lewis Lapham, John Leo, Anne Matthews, the Multicultural Management Fellows [sic] of the University of Missouri Journalism School, Judith S. Neaman and Carole G. Silver, the New York State Social Studies Review and Development Committee, Hugh Rawson, Jeff Sheshol, the Smith College Office of Student Affairs, John Taylor, Amoja Three Rivers, and—last but not least—the gang at the Modern Language Association introduced us to many important terms and concepts that might otherwise have escaped our attention.

The extraordinary scholarship and brilliant editorial innovations of linguists Cheris Kramarae and Paula Treichler, authors of *A Feminist Dictionary,* again and again proved invaluable. William Lutz's unique work as chair of the Committee on Public Doublespeak of the National Council of Teachers of English has also been a constant inspiration, and was indispensable to us as we compiled our section on bureaucratically suitable (BS) language. And we would be remiss if we did not acknowledge Dinesh D'Souza and Roger Kimball, not only for their groundbreaking research (generously supported by the John M. Olin Foundation and its president, former Treasury Secretary William Simon), but also for their zealous—if somewhat unexpected—proselytizing on behalf of traditional liberal values, even as others abandon them.

Needless to say, we owe a profound debt to those who have used, described, and, in many cases, coined the hundreds of individual words cataloged here. In a very real sense, they have created not just our dictionary but the remarkable new language that has made it necessary. These individuals are far too numerous to list in these acknowledgments, but their names may be found in the Source Notes at the end of the book.

Special thanks to Lauren Attinello and Tom Brannon, and to our longtime friend Michael Frith for leaping to the rescue when we needed help with illustrations. We are also grateful to Jordan Schapps, who took time off from his duties at *New York* magazine to art-direct our cover.

We're deeply appreciative of the invaluable help, advice, friendship, and support given us by our editor, David Rosenthal; our agent, Ed Victor; our designer, Robert Bull; and everyone associated with Random House and Villard Books who has aided and abetted our project—most notably Patricia Abdale, Richard Aquan, Jon Asmundsson, Lorraine DeMarino, Jacqueline Duval, Harry Evans, Leta Evanthes, Peter Gethers, Bernie Klein, Robert Legault, Maureen McMahon, Grace McQuade, Beth Pearson, Diane Reverand, Jamie Sims, Chris Stamey, and Janet Wygal.

And, finally, we must offer an apology to our culturally aware readers for including in the title of our book the phrase "politically correct," which, because it has been co-opted by the enemies of language reform as a label with which to belittle the multicultural movement, is alas itself no longer "politically correct."

PERMISSIONS ACKNOWLEDGMENTS

Grateful acknowledgment is made to the following for permission to reprint previously published material:

CROWN PUBLISHERS, INC.: Excerpts from *A Dictionary of Euphemisms and Other Doubletalk* by Hugh Rawson. Copyright © 1981 by Hugh Rawson. Reprinted by permission of Crown Publishers, Inc.

FACTS ON FILE, INC.: Excerpts from *Kind Words* by Judith Neaman and Carole Silver. Copyright © 1989 by Judith Neaman and Carole Silver. Reprinted by permission of Facts on File, Inc., New York.

HARPERCOLLINS PUBLISHERS, INC., AND WILLIAM LUTZ: Excerpts from *Doublespeak* by William Lutz. Copyright © 1989 by Blonde Bear, Inc. Reprinted by permission of the publisher, HarperCollins Publishers, Inc., and the author, William Lutz.

NEW YORK MAGAZINE: Excerpts from "Are You Politically Correct?" by John Taylor. Copyright © 1992 by K-III Magazine Corporation. All rights reserved. Reprinted by permission of *New York* magazine.

THE NEW YORK TIMES: Excerpts from "Brave, New 'Cruelty Free' World" by Anne Matthews. Copyright © 1991 by The New York Times Company. Reprinted by permission.

PANDORA PRESS: Excerpts from *A Feminist Dictionary* by Cheris Kramarae and Paula Treichler. Reprinted by permission of Pandora Press, a division of Unwin Hyman, of HarperCollins Publishers Limited (London).

AMOJA THREE RIVERS: Excerpts from *Cultural Etiquette: A Guide for the Well-Intentioned* by Amoja Three Rivers published in 1990 and 1991 by Market Wimmin, Box 28, Indian Valley, VA 24105.

U.S. NEWS & WORLD REPORT: Excerpts from "The new verbal order" by John Leo, July 22, 1991. Copyright © 1991 by *U.S. News & World Report*. Excerpts from "The political taboos of the '90's" by John Leo, March 4, 1991. Copyright © 1991 by *U.S. News & World Report*.

ILLUSTRATION CREDITS

AP/Wide World: pages 16, 17, 19, 21, 25 (top), 30 (top), 33, 34, 35, 39, 42 (top), 45 (bottom), 49, 51, 54, 56 (bottom), 57, 65, 71, 76, 83, 84 (top), 87 (top), 101, 103 (top), 105, 108, 117, 118, 132 (top), 133 (bottom)

Lauren Attinello: pages 25 (bottom), 42 (bottom), 52, 55, 56 (top), 75, 89 (top and middle), 91, 103 (bottom), 133 (top), 145

Tom Brannon: pages 45 (top), 60, 64 (top), 68, 84 (bottom), 87 (bottom), 94, 97, 100

British Trademarks of the 1920s & 1930s, by John Mendenhall, Chronicle Books, 1989: page 102.

Dover Publications: pages 6, 7, 8, 9, 38, 58, 61 (top and bottom), 67, 69, 89 (bottom), 90, 93, 96, 98 (top), 106, 107, 119, 132 (bottom), 134, 137, 148 (top)

Hoaxes, Humbugs, and Spectacles, by Mark Sloan, Villard Books, 1990: page 30 (bottom).

New York Public Library Picture Collection: pages 3, 20, 28, 44, 64 (bottom), 72, 80, 88, 95, 116, 122, 143, 148 (bottom)

Trademarks of the Forties & Fifties, by Eric Baker and Tyler Blik, Chronicle Books, 1988: page 19 (top).

ABOUT THE AUTHORS

Although HENRY BEARD is a typical product of elitist educational institutions and a beneficiary of a number of negative action programs, he has struggled to overcome his many severe privileges. He was a cofounder and one of the original editors of the implosional postmodernist periodical the *National Lampoon* and is the author of more than a dozen bestselling processed tree carcasses, including a series of deconstructionist dictionaries on the subjects of wind exploitation *(Sailing)*, turf murder *(Golfing)*, land rape for the benefit of ice people *(Skiing)*, the genocidal oppression of ichthyo-Americans *(Fishing)*, and the preparation of scorched animal corpses *(Cooking)*. He also wrote the landmark nonspeciocentric narratives *Miss Piggy's Guide to Life* and *French for Cats,* as well as the postancient classics *Latin for All Occasions* and *Latin for Even More Occasions.* He has previously co(labor)ated with Christopher Cerf on a pair of readerly—and writerly—texts, *The Pentagon Catalog,* and (with Sarah Durkee and Sean Kelly) the re-representational pastiche *The Book of Sequels.* His latest work is *The Official Exceptions to the Rules of Golf,* an antifoundationalist rescription of the canon of links behavior that he believes would make a dandy gift for Dad or grad this spring.

CHRISTOPHER CERF is a melanin-impoverished, temporarily abled, straight, half-Anglo-, half-Jewish-American male, a graduate of Harvard (a college categorized by former Dartmouth dean Gregory Ricks as "one of the slickest forms of genocide going"), and a multiple Grammy- and Emmy-winning contributor to the well-intentioned, but unabashedly assimilationist, television program *Sesame*

Street. He has spent most of his life trying, and failing, to atone for these shortcomings. Among his more notable efforts in this regard are: *Not the New York Times,* a dominant-culture newspaper parody that he conceived and coedited, whose surprising success resulted in the needless destruction of thousands of innocent trees; *The Experts Speak,* coedited with Victor Navasky, which, by purporting to prove that experts are wrong at least 50 percent of the time, created the misguided impression that there is such a thing as absolute truth; *The Gulf War Reader,* an anthology of readings about Operation Desert Storm, coedited with Micah Sifry, which, in its attempt to provide a balanced picture, veered dangerously toward accommodationism; *Free to Be…a Family,* coedited with Marlo Thomas, which was intended as a celebration of the diversity of the American family but ended up infuriating antihierarchists by reaching the number one spot on *The New York Times* bestseller list; and *The Book of Sequels,* coauthored with Henry Beard, Sarah Durkee, and Sean Kelly, in which Cerf and his colleagues not only unaccountably praised canonical works, but also shamelessly appropriated the creations of others for their own benefit.

ABOUT THE AMERICAN HYPHEN SOCIETY

THE AMERICAN HYPHEN SOCIETY is a community-based, not-for-profit, grass-roots consciousness-raising/education-research alliance that seeks to help effectuate the across-the-board self-empowerment of wide-ranging culture-, nationality-, ethnicity-, creed-, gender-, and sexual-orientation-defined identity groups by excising all multi-culturally-less-than-sensitive terminology from the English language, and replacing it with counter-hegemonic, cruelty-, gender-, bias-, and, if necessary, content-free speech. The society's motto is "It became necessary to destroy the language in order to save it." Its headquarters are in Wilkes-Barre, Pennsylvania.

In connection with its ongoing program of updating and revising its reference publications, the Society invites its readers to submit appropriate terms and phrases too new, or too obscure, to have appeared in the current edition of *The Official Politically Correct Dictionary and Handbook*. Please send all proposed entries, complete with source information if available, to the American Hyphen Society, in care of our publishers, Villard Books, 201 East 50th Street, New York, New York 10022. Since we will be unable to return your submissions, we request that they be written with non-toxic ink on acid-free paper, so that any unusable ones may be promptly and safely recycled.